Reading & Writing
Sahara

NATIONAL GEOGRAPHIC
LEARNING

Australia • Brazil • Mexico • Singapore • United Kingdom • United States

NATIONAL GEOGRAPHIC
L E A R N I N G

National Geographic Learning,
a Cengage Company

Reading & Writing, Sahara

**Lauri Blass, Mari Vargo, Keith S. Folse,
April Muchmore-Vokoun, Elena Vestri**

Publisher: Sherrise Roehr

Executive Editor: Laura LeDréan

Managing Editor: Jennifer Monaghan

Digital Implementation Manager,
Irene Boixareu

Senior Media Researcher: Leila Hishmeh

Director of Global Marketing: Ian Martin

Regional Sales and National Account
Manager: Andrew O'Shea

Content Project Manager: Ruth Moore

Senior Designer: Lisa Trager

Manufacturing Planner: Mary Beth
Hennebury

Composition: Lumina Datamatics

For permission to use material from this text or product,
submit all requests online at **cengage.com/permissions**
Further permissions questions can be emailed to
permissionrequest@cengage.com

Student Edition: Reading & Writing, Sahara
ISBN-13: 978-0-357-13831-1

National Geographic Learning
20 Channel Center Street
Boston, MA 02210
USA

Locate your local office at **international.cengage.com/region**

Visit National Geographic Learning online at **ELTNGL.com**
Visit our corporate website at **www.cengage.com**

Printed in China
Print Number: 02 Print Year: 2019

PHOTO CREDITS

1 Wes C. Skiles/National Geographic Creative, 5 Dan Wiklund/Getty Images, 6 petekarici/Getty Images, 8 Burt Silverman/National Geographic Creative, 9 Martin Edström/National Geographic Creative, 12-13 Wes C. Skiles/National Geographic Creative, 14 Alejandro Tumas/National Geographic, 15 Anadolu Agency/Getty Images, 19 Joel Sartore/National Geographic Photo Ark, 22-23 © Richard Nowitz/National Geographic Creative, 24 © Steve Vidler/Alamy, 28: © JASON EDWARDS/National Geographic Creative, 29: © Todd Shoemake/Shutterstock.com, 31: © Doug Menuez/Photodisc/getty images, 42: © E.J.Baumeister Jr./Alamy, 44: © SZ Photo/Scherl/DIZ/Muenchen GmbH, Sueddeutsche/Zeitung Photo/Alamy, 49 Jens Schlueter/Getty Images, 50-51 Lam Yik Fei/Getty Images, 53 © Erik Jepsen/Calit2/UCSD, 54 Sarah Parcak/National Geographic Creative, 57 Mike Hennig/National Geographic Creative, 60-61 © Dmitri Alexander, 63 © Ben Keene, 69 David Doubilet/National Geographic Creative, 70 (br) Hannele Lahti/National Geographic, 70-71 (c) Jason Edwards/National Geographic, 71 (tl) Richard Folwell/Science Photo Library/Getty Images, (c) Paul Chesley/National Geographic, (bl) David Doubilet/National Geographic Creative, 73 Brian J. Skerry/National Geographic Creative, 74 Roberto Caccuri/Contrasto/Redux, 77 Brian J. Skerry/National Geographic Creative, 80 (tr) Mark Thissen/National Geographic Creative, 80-81 (b) Mariel Furlong/Alejandro Tumas/National Geographic Image Collection

Scope and Sequence

Unit Title and Theme	Reading Texts and Video	ACADEMIC SKILLS Reading
1 **EXPLORATION** *page 1* ACADEMIC TRACK: Earth Science	**Reading 1** Secret Cities **VIDEO** The Lost World **Reading 2** Into the Unknown	**Focus** Identifying Facts and Speculations Predicting, Understanding Main Ideas and Details, Understanding Purpose, Summarizing

Unit Title and Theme	Writing	Grammar for Writing
2 **DESCRIPTIVE PARAGRAPHS** *page 22*	What Is a Descriptive Paragraph? Describing with the Five Senses Using Positive and Negative Adjectives for More Precise Meanings	Using Adjectives in Writing Using Prepositions of Location to Describe Using Correct Word Order with Prepositions of Location

Unit Title and Theme	Reading Texts and Video	ACADEMIC SKILLS Reading
3 **CONNECTED LIVES** *page 49* ACADEMIC TRACK: Communications / Sociology	**Reading 1** The Power of Crowd **VIDEO** Citizen Scientists **Reading 2** Internet Island	**Focus** Taking Notes (Part 1) Predicting, Understanding the Main Idea(s), Identifying Details, Understanding a Process, Sequencing

Unit Title and Theme	Reading Texts and Video	ACADEMIC SKILLS Reading
4 **SAVING OUR SEAS** *page 69* ACADEMIC TRACK: Environmental Science	**Reading 1** Where Have All the Fish Gone? **VIDEO** Saving Bluefin Tuna **Reading 2** What We Eat Makes a Difference	**Focus** Interpreting Visual Information Predicting, Understanding the Main Idea(s), Understanding a Process, Identifying Problems and Solutions, Identifying Opinions

Critical Thinking	Writing	Vocabulary Extension
Focus Understanding Analogies Applying, Analyzing	**Skill Focus** Introducing Examples **Language for Writing** Expressing Interests and Desires **Writing Goal** Writing a paragraph about a place worth exploring	**Word Forms** Adjectives and Nouns for Measurement **Word Partners** *run* + adverb/preposition

Building Better Vocabulary	Original Student Writing	
Word Associations Using Collocations	**Original Student Writing** Write a paragraph that describes something. **Photo Topic:** Describe a national monument that is important to you. **Timed Writing Topic:** Describe your ideal teacher.	

Critical Thinking	Writing	Vocabulary Extension
Focus Making Inferences Reflecting, Analyzing	**Skill Focus** Writing a Concluding Sentence **Language for Writing** Using the Present Perfect Tense **Writing Goal** Writing a descriptive paragraph about a crowdsourcing project	**Word Partners** adjective + *contribution* **Word Link** *-al*

Critical Thinking		Vocabulary Extension
Focus Evaluating an Argument Synthesizing, Reflecting		**Word Forms** Changing Nouns into Adjectives **Word Partners** verb + *on*

NOTES

EXPLORATION 1

A diver finds a cow's skull in an underwater cave in Yucatán, Mexico.

THINK AND DISCUSS

1 Do you know of any famous explorers? What do/did they do?

2 What places would you like to explore?

A Look at the information on these pages and answer the questions.

1. What is the Mariana Trench? What is special about it?
2. Who has successfully traveled to the bottom of the Mariana Trench alone?

B Match the words in blue to their definitions.

_____ (v) to be in a particular place

_____ (v) to go through something and know how it feels

_____ (adj) far down from the top or surface

240 meters

average U.S. navy submarine

1,500 meters

elephant seal

EXPLORING THE MARIANA TRENCH

Located in the Pacific Ocean about 300 kilometers off Guam, the Mariana Trench is the deepest place in the world. It is like a deep valley. The deepest point—Challenger Deep—is about 11 kilometers below the ocean surface.

In 2012, film director James Cameron became the first person to experience traveling alone to Challenger Deep. Traveling in a submarine—*Deepsea Challenger*—he explored the bottom for more than two hours, taking videos and collecting samples.

Ocean Surface

30 meters

scuba diver

1,000 meters

1,000 meters

No sunlight beyond this point

2,000 meters

2,000 meters

sperm whale

3,000 meters

3,800 meters

4,000 meters

wreck of the RMS *Titanic*

5,000 meters

6,000 meters

MOUNT EVEREST

7,000 meters

If Mount Everest were underwater, it would not reach the bottom of the trench.

8,000 meters

8,848 meters

9,000 meters

Deepsea Challenger

10,000 meters

10,898 meters

Challenger Deep

11,000 meters

Reading 1

PREPARING TO READ

BUILDING VOCABULARY **A** The words in **blue** below are used in the reading passage on pages 5–6. Read the paragraph. Then match the correct form of each word to its definition.

Many archaeologists dream of being able to **discover** a lost city. In 2017, that dream became a reality for a team of archaeologists in Honduras. They were the first people to explore a remote **region** of the Central American rain forest. The team found the remains of a **massive** pyramid **hidden** in the jungle. It also identified more than 50 stone sculptures in the pyramid; many more objects may be buried **underground**. The **artifacts** are thought to be over a thousand years old, and belong to an **ancient** culture that disappeared long ago.

1. _____ (n) area

2. _____ (v) to find

3. _____ (adj) very old

4. _____ (adj) very large

5. _____ (adj) not easy to see

6. _____ (adj) below the surface of the Earth

7. _____ (n) an object that people made a long time ago

USING VOCABULARY **B** Discuss these questions with a partner.

1. Are there any places in your city that are **underground**? What are they?

2. Which **region** of your country do you live in? Are there any other regions of your country you would like to visit?

PREDICTING **C** Look at the photo and the title of the reading passage on page 5. What kind of "secret cities" do you think are described in the passage? What do you think they were used for? Discuss your ideas with a partner.

_____

_____

I think the cities are probably …   *They might be used for … because …*

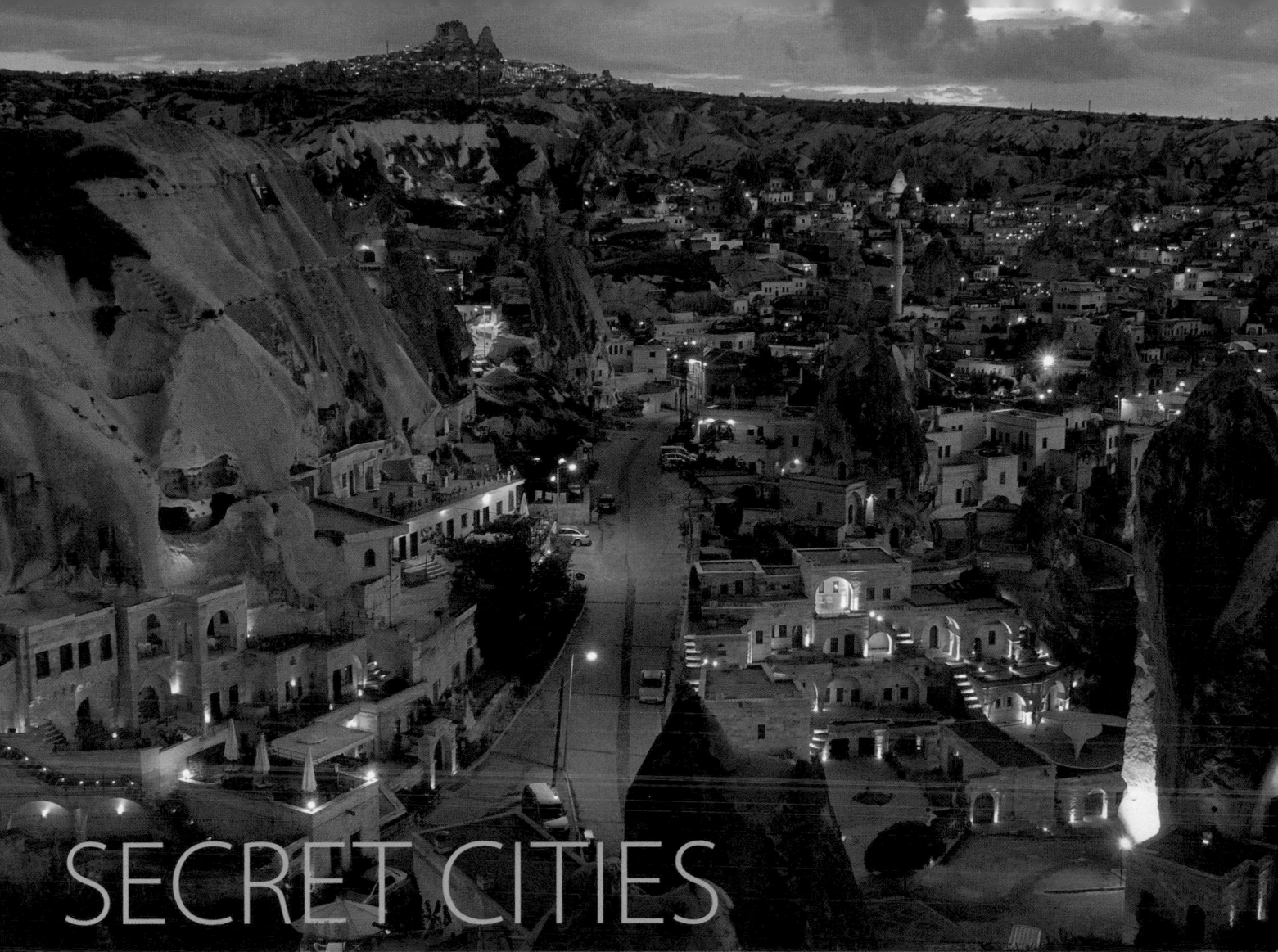

SECRET CITIES

🎧 Track 1

A   In 1963, a resident of the Cappadocia region of Turkey was doing some renovations[1] on his house. When he knocked down one of his walls, he was surprised to find a hidden room carved into the stone. He explored the room, and found that it led to an underground city—the city of Derinkuyu.

B   The underground city is over 60 meters deep—deep enough for a 20-story building. It contains massive stone doors that could only be opened or closed from the inside. This piece of evidence leads experts to believe that the underground city was built to protect the city's residents from enemies. More than 20,000 people could hide inside it. Over 600 doors lead to the city, hidden under and around existing homes.

C   The hidden city had its own religious centers, livestock stables,[2] kitchens, and even schools. Wells, water tanks, and at least 15,000 air shafts[3] made the city a comfortable place. However, experts are not sure exactly how old the underground city is, because any records of its construction and use have disappeared.

[1] renovations: works that improve the design or condition of a house or building
[2] stable: a place to keep horses and cows
[3] shaft: an opening that goes all the way through a building

▲ Rock formations called "fairy chimneys" can be found throughout the Cappadocia region in Turkey.

D   Until recently, Derinkuyu was the largest known underground city in Cappadocia. In 2013, however, construction workers **discovered** another underground city during the building of a housing project. This city—**located** beneath the city of Nevşehir—is one of the largest known underground cities in the world. According to researchers, this newly discovered **ancient** city could cover over 450,000 square meters and is over 110 meters deep. This means that using only simple tools, the ancient builders dug an area big enough for 65 soccer fields, and deep enough to contain a 35-story building!

E   Researchers have found **artifacts** in this city such as tools and bowls. These artifacts suggest that the city is probably up to 5,000 years old. Like Derinkuyu, it was probably built as a place where people could stay safe during times of war.

F   In the future, other people may **experience** the same excitement that the homeowner and the construction workers felt. There are already more than 30 known underground cities in the Cappadocia region, but experts believe there may be more than 200. So there are likely to be other hidden wonders, just waiting to be discovered.

▼ **Visitors exploring the underground city of Derinkuyu**

UNDERSTANDING THE READING

A Match each paragraph (A–F) to its main idea.

UNDERSTANDING MAIN IDEAS

1. _____ There are likely to be many more underground cities in Turkey that have not yet been found.
2. _____ Scientists don't know how old the city is, but it seemed to have enough resources for its people.
3. _____ A man in Turkey discovered something surprising beneath his house.
4. _____ The artifacts found in the city below Nevşehir helped scientists work out its age and purpose.
5. _____ The structure of the hidden city suggests that people used the underground city to hide from danger.
6. _____ Workers found an underground city in Turkey that was bigger than Derinkuyu.

B Complete the chart about the two underground cities in Turkey. If the information is not in the reading, write "not given."

UNDERSTANDING DETAILS

	Derinkuyu	below Nevşehir
Where is it located?		
Who discovered it?	a resident in the city	
How deep is it?		
How old is it?		
How many people could live there?		
What might be the purpose of the city?		

> **CRITICAL THINKING**   When writers make an **analogy**, they compare something to another thing that is easier to understand. For example, to help a reader imagine the length of a blue whale, writers could say "A blue whale is about 24 meters long—around the length of two buses."

C Look back at paragraphs B and D in the reading passage. Find an analogy in each paragraph and underline it. What does each analogy help the reader understand?

CRITICAL THINKING: UNDERSTANDING ANALOGIES

Paragraph B: the **depth** / **area** of the city

Paragraph D: the **area** / **volume** and **depth** / **age** of the city

D Look back at paragraph E in the reading passage. What analogy could you use to describe the age of the city? Discuss your ideas with a partner.

CRITICAL THINKING: APPLYING

That's as old as …   *That's older than …*

DEVELOPING READING SKILLS

CATEGORIZING **A** Read the paragraph about Ibn Battuta below. Then decide whether each piece of information is a fact (F) or speculation (S).

Ibn Battuta was one of the world's greatest explorers. He was born in 1304 in Tangier, Morocco. At the age of 21, he left home to travel across unexplored parts of Africa and Asia. His journey took him to places such as Cairo, Iraq, and Delhi. He may also have visited Beijing around 1346, although some historians think this is unlikely. After traveling almost 120,000 kilometers over a period of 29 years, he returned to Morocco and told people of his travels. We know little about Battuta's life after he stopped traveling—some say he may have worked as a judge. Battuta probably died in 1368 or 1369, and his final resting place is unknown.

Ibn Battuta (right) on a visit to Mongolia

1. where Battuta was from   F   S

2. how old Battuta was when he left home   F   S

3. whether Battuta visited Beijing   F   S

4. how many years Battuta traveled   F   S

5. how Battuta lived after returning home   F   S

6. when Battuta died   F   S

CATEGORIZING **B** Look back at the reading passage on pages 5–6. Decide whether each of the following pieces of information is a fact (F) or speculation (S).

1. the year Derinkuyu's underground city was discovered   F   S

2. who discovered the underground cities   F   S

3. the age of the underground cities   F   S

4. why the two underground cities were built   F   S

5. the number of underground cities in Cappadocia   F   S

Video

National Geographic Explorer
Martin Edström and an assistant
photographer in Son Doong cave

THE LOST WORLD

BEFORE VIEWING

A Work with a partner. Read the title and look at the photo. How big do you think the cave is? Use an analogy to describe your ideas.

PREDICTING

B Read the information about Son Doong. Then answer the questions.

LEARNING ABOUT THE TOPIC

At more than five kilometers long, Son Doong is one of the largest caves in the world. The cave—located in Vietnam—was created millions of years ago when river water caused the rock under the mountain to become soft and fall apart. A man called Ho Khanh discovered Son Doong in 1991, but he didn't know how to enter it. As a result, the cave remained a mystery. In 2009, a team of British cavers began to explore Son Doong with the help of Ho Khanh. A year later, a different team of cavers visited, and became the first people to explore the entire length of the cave.

1. Where is the cave? _____

2. Is the cave natural or man-made? _____

3. Who were the first people to enter the cave? _____

4. What do you think explorers might find in the cave? _____

_____

C The words in **bold** below are used in the video. Read the sentences. Then match each word to its definition.

> The Mariana Trench is a **vast** underwater valley.
>
> A country's traditional art and music are usually an important part of its **heritage**.
>
> As a result of globalization, small businesses may be under **threat** from international companies.

1. _____ (adj) very wide or big

2. _____ (n) a possibility of something bad happening

3. _____ (n) something from the past that still has cultural importance

WHILE VIEWING

A ▶ Watch the video. Why does Edström want to take pictures of the cave? Circle the most suitable answer.

   a. to encourage more tourists to visit the cave

   b. to help future explorers find their way through it

   c. to make people aware of the cave so they will want to protect it

B ▶ Watch the video again. Answer the questions (1–4).

1. What is true about the pictures Edström and his team took?

   a. They show the cave from all angles.   b. They were taken using a flying robot.

2. What is an example of a dangerous thing the team had to do?

   a. avoid snakes   b. cross a river in the dark

3. Why is one of the sinkholes called "Watch out for dinosaurs"?

   a. Dinosaur bones were found there.   b. The area seemed like a different world.

4. What have scientists discovered in the cave?

   a. new types of insects and fish   b. evidence of early humans

AFTER VIEWING

A Discuss these questions with a partner.

1. Would you like to visit Son Doong? Why or why not?

2. What are some advantages and disadvantages of allowing tourists to visit the cave?

B Work with a partner. What analogy was mentioned in the video caption? What did it describe?

The analogy described the **size / age / importance** of the cave by stating that

_____ could

_____ .

Reading 2

PREPARING TO READ

A The words in **blue** below are used in the reading passage on pages 12–13. Read the paragraph. Then match the correct form of each word to its definition.

BUILDING VOCABULARY

Scientists have always been interested in knowing if life **exists** outside of Earth. The **universe** is **extremely** large, so there is a chance that there could be other forms of life. In 2017, scientists found seven Earth-size planets located 40 light years away. This discovery may bring us closer to answering the question of life beyond Earth.

1. _____ (adv) very, really

2. _____ (v) to live or be present in a particular place

3. _____ (n) everything that is in space, such as stars and planets

B Complete the sentences using the words in the box. Use a dictionary to help you.

BUILDING VOCABULARY

run out	challenging	creatures	risk	surface

1. Underwater cave exploration can be _____ and dangerous, and divers often _____ their lives on expeditions.

2. Divers have to come back up to the _____ before they _____ of oxygen.

3. The bottom of the Mariana Trench is completely dark and very cold, but there are some _____ that are able to live there.

C Discuss these questions with a partner.

USING VOCABULARY

1. Do you think that life might **exist** on other planets in the **universe**? If so, what kind of life do you think could exist?

2. What are some places that are **extremely** difficult to live in? Why?

D Look at the photo and read the first paragraph of the reading on pages 12–13. What are some challenges blue hole explorers could face? Discuss with a partner. Then check your ideas as you read the passage.

PREDICTING

_____

_____

_____

INTO THE UNKNOWN

🎧 Track 2

A In the early 19th century, much of the world was still unexplored. Today, most places on the **surface** of the Earth have been mapped. Some places, however, are still waiting to be discovered. Some of these are underground, in deep caves called blue holes.

B A blue hole is a special kind of underwater cave. It can be found inland[1] or in the sea. The hole forms when the earth above a cave falls in and water fills the space. Some of the world's most spectacular[2] blue holes are located in the Bahamas. The islands there may have more than a thousand blue holes. Blue holes can be very deep. For example, Dean's Blue Hole, one of the deepest blue holes in the world, is over 200 meters deep.

C An inland blue hole's water is very still and has different layers. A layer of fresh rainwater floats on top of salt water. The fresh water keeps oxygen from the atmosphere from reaching the salt water. Brightly colored bacteria live where the two layers meet.

D Diving into blue holes is **extremely** dangerous. Near the top of a blue hole, there is a layer of poisonous gas. This gas causes itching, dizziness, and—in large amounts—death. Divers must also be fast. They have to get in and out of a cave before their oxygen **runs out**. Additionally, it is very dark in these caves, so it is very easy to get lost. Divers therefore have to follow a guideline[3] as they swim through a blue hole. If they lose the guideline, they may not find their way back out of the cave.

E If blue holes are so dangerous, why do explorers and scientists **risk** their lives to explore them? One reason is that these

underwater caves can provide valuable scientific information. They provide clues about geology, archaeology, and biology. For example, some blue hole creatures, such as the remipede, probably haven't changed for millions of years.

The blue holes could even provide clues about astrobiology—the study of life in the universe. For example, divers have found bacteria there that can live without oxygen. Astrobiologist Kevin Hand says the bacteria in blue holes may be similar to forms of life that might exist on Jupiter's fourth largest moon, Europa. Similar life forms probably existed on Earth billions of years ago. "Our study of life's extremes on Earth," he says, can help increase

"our understanding of habitable environments off Earth."

In addition, the oxygen-free environment of the blue holes preserves bones of humans and animals that fell into the caves long ago. By studying blue holes, we can understand what life was like in prehistoric[4] times. As cave diver Kenny Broad says, "I can think of no other environment on Earth that is so challenging to explore and gives us back so much scientifically."

[1]inland: away from the ocean
[2]spectacular: very impressive or dramatic
[3]guideline: a line or a rope that someone follows to go from one place to another
[4]prehistoric: (people and things) existing at a time before information was written down

UNDERSTANDING THE READING

A Match each section of the passage to its purpose.

_____ 1. Paragraphs A–B   a. to explain the importance of studying blue holes

_____ 2. Paragraph C   b. to show why blue hole exploration is challenging

_____ 3. Paragraph D   c. to describe the structure of a blue hole

_____ 4. Paragraphs E–G   d. to explain what blue holes are and how they are formed

SUMMARIZING **B** Circle the correct words to complete the summary about blue holes.

Blue holes are caves that are [1] **underwater / high up in the mountains**. They were formed millions of years ago when [2] **huge earthquakes happened / the land above them fell in** and water entered the space. Blue holes are located on land or in the sea. Many of them are very deep and the water inside the holes is usually very [3] **rough / calm**. Although exploring blue holes is dangerous, many scientists still risk their lives to dive into them. They think that blue holes can tell us a lot about [4] **ancient life forms / how the oceans were formed**.

UNDERSTANDING DETAILS **C** Complete the labels with information about an inland blue hole.

1. At the top of the blue hole is a layer of _____ water, while below it is a layer of _____ water. The top layer blocks _____ from entering the blue hole.

2. The gas near the top of the blue hole is _____, and breathing in too much of it can sometimes lead to _____.

3. _____ live in between the top and bottom layers.

4. It is very _____ in this part of a blue hole, so divers need to use a _____ when swimming.

CRITICAL THINKING: ANALYZING **D** Look back at the reading passage on pages 12–13. Decide whether each piece of information is a fact (F) or speculation (S). Then discuss your ideas with a partner.

		F	S
1.	how blue holes are formed	F	S
2.	the depth of Dean's Blue Hole	F	S
3.	what the remipede looked like in the past	F	S
4.	the types of life that we can find on Europa	F	S
5.	the amount of oxygen in blue holes	F	S

Writing

EXPLORING WRITTEN ENGLISH

NOTICING

A Complete the sentences with the correct form of the verb in parentheses. Then underline the expressions that show an interest in or a desire to do something.

1. I would love to _____ (discover) a lost city someday.

2. I would like to _____ (study) archaeology because I want to _____ (learn) about ancient history.

3. I would be interested in _____ (visit) Turkey someday because I want to _____ (see) the underground cities.

4. I want to _____ (take) a tour of Paris and see the Louvre Museum.

5. I would be interested in _____ (learn) Spanish because I want to _____ (visit) Central America.

LANGUAGE FOR WRITING Expressing Interests and Desires

You can use certain expressions to introduce what you want to do. These include:

I would like to …   *I would love to …*

I want to …   *I would be interested in …*

Use the base form of the verb after *I would like to / I would love to*, and *I want to*. Use a gerund (*-ing* verb) after *I would be interested in*.

*I **would like to explore** the blue holes of the Bahamas because they look very interesting.*

*I **would love to go** to Central America because I'm interested in Mayan history.*

*I **would be interested in going** there because I am learning Spanish and I want to improve my Spanish language skills.*

▼ **The site of one of Turkey's underground cities**

B Complete the chart with things you want to do in the next five years. Give reasons for each one.

Things you want to do	Two reasons why
visit Greece	1. see the ancient temples 2. eat Mediterranean food
1.	1. 2.
2.	1. 2.
3.	1. 2.

Use your notes in the chart above to write a sentence about each of the things that you want to do. Use the phrases in the Language for Writing box to help you.

Example:

I would like to visit Greece because I want to see the ancient temples and eat Mediterranean food.

1. _____

   _____

   _____

2. _____

   _____

   _____

3. _____

   _____

   _____

WRITING SKILL Introducing Examples

You can give examples to give more information about your supporting ideas. You learned how to identify examples (*for example, for instance*). Here are more phrases that introduce examples:

To give an example, …

A famous/great example is …

One of the best examples is …

Sometimes, people use the short form "e.g." in their writing to introduce an example. You can use this in informal writing—such as in an email to a friend—but it may not always be appropriate in academic writing.

Note: You have learned to order and connect supporting ideas in a paragraph using *also*, *in addition*, and *finally*. You can use these words and phrases in this unit to organize your supporting ideas.

C Read the paragraph below. Use the phrases in the box to link supporting ideas and introduce examples.

a famous example	first of all	for instance	in addition

I would like to explore Australia for many reasons. ¹ _____ , there are a lot of interesting animals in Australia. I would love to see some of the amazing animals that live on the south coast. ² _____ is the fairy penguin, the world's smallest species of penguin. ³ _____ , Australia is a good place to study aboriginal culture. The Art Gallery of New South Wales, ⁴ _____ , has an excellent collection of aboriginal art.

D Choose one thing you would like to do from exercise B. Expand on your sentence in B to include examples. Use the expressions from the Writing Skill box to help you.

Example:

I would like to visit Greece because I want to see the ancient temples. For example, I would love to see the Temple of Apollo at Delphi. I also really want to eat Mediterranean food, such as moussaka.

_____

_____

_____

_____

_____

_____

WRITING TASK

> **GOAL** You are going to write a paragraph about the following topic:
> Where would you most like to explore? Why would you like to go there?

BRAINSTORMING **A** Make a list of places you would like to explore or learn more about. Discuss your list with a partner.

_____

_____

_____

PLANNING **B** Follow these steps to make notes for your paragraph. Don't worry about grammar or spelling. Don't write complete sentences.

Step 1 Look at your brainstorming notes. Circle one place you want to write about.

Step 2 Write a topic sentence stating the place you are interested in going to.

Step 3 Think of three reasons that you want to explore this place. Note them in the outline as your supporting ideas.

Step 4 Think of an example or an explanation for each reason. Note them as your details.

OUTLINE

Topic sentence: _____

_____

Supporting Idea 1: _____

_____

Detail: _____

Supporting Idea 2: _____

_____

Detail: _____

Supporting Idea 3: _____

_____

Detail: _____

FIRST DRAFT **C** Use the information in the outline to write a first draft of your paragraph.

REVISING PRACTICE

The drafts below are similar to the one you are going to write.

What did the writer do in Draft 2 to improve the paragraph? Match the changes (a–d) to the highlighted parts.

a. expanded on an example
b. fixed an error with expressing an interest or a desire
c. added a linking expression to order ideas
d. added an expression for introducing an example

Draft 1

I would like to explore Australia for many reasons. First of all, there are many beautiful and unusual birds there. There are bright red and blue rosellas, a type of Australian parrot. It is a great place to go diving. A famous example is the Great Barrier Reef, which is filled with beautiful fish. Finally, I'm interested in learn more about the aboriginal culture of Australia. For instance, I would like to visit the Australia Museum in Sydney.

Draft 2

I would like to explore Australia for many reasons. First of all, there are many beautiful and unusual birds there. To give an example, ☐ there are bright red and blue rosellas, a type of Australian parrot. Second, it is a great place to go diving. A famous example is ☐ the Great Barrier Reef, which is filled with beautiful fish. Finally, I'm interested in learning more about the aboriginal culture of ☐ Australia. For instance, I would like to visit the Australia Museum in Sydney because it is one of the best places to see aboriginal art ☐ and artifacts.

D Now use the questions below to revise your paragraph.

REVISED DRAFT

- ☐ Did you use the correct expression for stating where you want to go?
- ☐ Did you use linking expressions for your supporting ideas?
- ☐ Did you include a detail for each supporting idea?
- ☐ Did you use the correct expressions for introducing examples?

◀ a rosella

EDITING PRACTICE

Read the information below.

In sentences expressing interest or desire, remember to:

- use the base form of the verb after *would like to, would love to,* and *want to*.
- use a gerund after *be interested in*.

Correct one mistake with language for expressing interest in each of the sentences (1–5).

1. I would like visit the Amazon rain forest because there are many different types of animals there.

2. I would love to exploring New York City because it is full of interesting art and culture.

3. My brother and I are interested in to visit Russia because we want to learn more about Russian history.

4. My sister would like traveling to every continent because she loves to learn about different cultures.

5. My parents would like to go to Turkey one day because they want to exploring the underground cities.

FINAL DRAFT **E** **Follow these steps to write a final draft.**

1. Check your revised draft for mistakes with language for expressing interest.

2. Now use the checklist on page 88 to write a final draft. Make any other necessary changes.

UNIT REVIEW

Answer the following questions.

1. Which place mentioned in this unit would you be most interested in exploring? Why?

_____

_____

_____

2. What are some words that show that something is a speculation?

_____

_____

_____

3. Do you remember the meanings of these words? Check (✓) the ones you know. Look back at the unit and review the ones you don't know.

Reading 1:

☐ ancient	☐ artifact	☐ deep
☐ discover	☐ experience	☐ hidden
☐ located **AWL**	☐ massive	☐ region **AWL**
☐ underground		

Reading 2:

☐ challenging **AWL**	☐ creature	☐ exist
☐ extremely	☐ risk	☐ run out
☐ surface	☐ universe	

NOTES

Descriptive Paragraphs

The illuminated Jefferson Memorial
is located is Washington, D.C.

OBJECTIVES To learn how to write a descriptive paragraph
To practice describing with the five senses
To learn about adjectives; positive and negative adjectives;
prepositions of location

Can you describe an important monument you know well?

What Is a Descriptive Paragraph?

A descriptive paragraph describes how something or someone looks or feels. It gives an impression of something. If, for example, you only wanted to write specific information about a certain river, you could write a paragraph filled with facts about the river. However, if you wanted to tell about the feelings you had when you sailed on a boat on the same river, you would write a descriptive paragraph.

A descriptive paragraph:

- describes
- gives impressions, not definitions
- "shows" the reader
- creates a sensory* image in the reader's mind

*related to the five senses: hearing, taste, touch, sight, and smell

ACTIVITY 1 Studying a Descriptive Paragraph

Discuss the Preview Questions with your classmates. Then read the example paragraph and answer the questions that follow.

Preview Questions

1. What are the top five adjectives that come to mind when you try to describe a very busy place?

2. How are the busiest street and river you have ever seen in person similar?

The Sights and Sounds of the Chao Phraya River

On our trip to Bangkok last year, my friends and I took a boat trip on the Chao Phraya River, which is the **principal** river of Thailand. This busy river is **crowded** with river buses, water taxis, fishing boats, and tourist boats. Every day local people use these boats because they are faster than the thousands of cars that overfill Bangkok's busy streets. Our river boat was so crowded that we could hardly move, yet we seemed to fly down the river, enjoying the cool breeze. The scenery along the shore surprised me. My mind had a hard time accepting the sight of **massive**, brand-new **skyscrapers** and tall modern hotels so near the beautiful golden palaces and temples that are more than 200 years old. While the city of Bangkok is loud from the noise of so many cars, the river is actually peaceful **in spite of** all the boat activity. I will never forget the beautiful red sun setting as we arrived at our final **destination**. Because of all the things I experienced that day on our trip, I highly recommend that you take a boat trip along the Chao Phraya River.

principal: main, most important

crowded: with many people

massive: huge

a skyscraper: very tall building that seems to touch the sky

in spite of: although, regardless of

the destination: the place you are traveling to

Post-Reading

1. What words did the writer use to describe the river?

_____

_____

2. How did the author feel during the ride?

_____

_____

3. What other information would you like to know about this trip?

_____

_____

Describing with the Five Senses

Good writers use words that appeal to some or all of the five senses—sight, taste, touch, hearing, and smell—to help describe a topic. Here is a list of the senses and examples of what they can describe. Add examples of your own.

Sense	Example 1	Example 2
sight	a sunset	_____
taste	a chocolate cake	_____
touch	silk	_____
hearing	a baby's cry	_____
smell	a perfume	_____

ACTIVITY 2 **Using Adjectives to Describe Sensory Information**

In the left column, write your five examples from your list above. In the right column, write three adjectives that describe each object. Try to use different senses.

Example	Description
sunset	purple, streaked, majestic
1. _____	_____
2. _____	_____
3. _____	_____
4. _____	_____
5. _____	_____

ACTIVITY 3 **Writing Sentences Using Sensory Adjectives**

Use the five examples from Activity 2 to write five descriptive sentences. Use each example item as the topic of one of the sentences and include one or more of the adjectives you wrote. Share your sentences with a classmate.

1. The majestic sunset warmed the sky with orange and purple streaks.

   _____

2. _____

   _____

3. _____

_____

4. _____

_____

5. _____

_____

ACTIVITY 4   Studying Example Descriptive Paragraphs

Discuss the Preview Questions with your classmates. Then read the example paragraphs and answer the questions that follow.

Descriptive Paragraph 1

This first paragraph describes the sights, smells, and sounds of a subway station.

Preview Questions

1. What is a subway? Where do you usually find a subway?

2. What kinds of people use the subway?

3. Have you ever been on a subway? How did you feel when you rode on it? Can you recall what you saw, smelled, and heard?

Example Paragraph 2

Underground Events

The subway is an attack on your senses. You walk down the steep, **smelly** staircase onto the subway **platform**. On the far right wall, a broken clock shows that the time is four-thirty. You wonder how long it has been broken. A mother and her crying child are standing to your left. She is trying to clean dried chocolate **syrup** off the child's messy face. **Farther** to the left, two old men are **arguing** about the most recent tax increase. You hear a little noise and see some paper trash roll by like a soccer ball. The most interesting thing you see while you are waiting for your subway train is a poster. It reads, "Come to Jamaica." Deep blue skies, a lone palm tree, and **sapphire** waters call you to this exotic place, which is so far from where you actually are.

smelly: smelling bad or unpleasant

a platform: a raised area

a syrup: a thick liquid

farther: comparative form of the word *far*

to argue: to fight verbally

sapphire: dark blue color like the color of a sapphire gemstone

Post-Reading

1. From the information in this paragraph, how do you think the writer feels about the subway?

   _____

2. Which of the five senses does the writer use to describe this place? Give examples from the paragraph to support your answer.

   _____

   _____

   _____

   _____

   _____

3. What verb tense is used in this paragraph? Why do you think the writer uses that tense?

   _____

   _____

Descriptive Paragraph 2

The paragraph on the next page describes a memory about a dangerous storm.

Preview Questions

1. What are some dangerous kinds of weather?

2. Have you ever experienced these kinds of weather? How did you feel?

3. When you think of these kinds of weather, what sensory adjectives come to mind?

Danger from the Sky

The long, **slender tornado** began to **descend** from the **spinning** clouds and started its horrible destruction. When the deadly storm finally touched the ground, many things were already flying in the air. The tornado **ripped** the roof from an old house and threw the contents of the home across the neighborhood. The tornado used its power to grab huge trees and toss cars around as if they were toys. Power lines and traffic lights were also victims of its deadly power. All the while, the tornado's extreme winds **roared** like a wild animal. It was hard to believe that something that looked so **delicate** could cause so much destruction.

slender: thin, narrow (positive adjective)

a tornado: a rotating column of air that moves at very high speeds

to descend: to move downwards

spinning: moving in a circle

to rip: to tear violently and quickly

to roar: to make a loud and deep sound

delicate: fragile

Post-Reading

1. What does this paragraph describe?

   _____

   _____

2. What verb tense does the writer use in this paragraph? _____

   Choose five verbs and change them to the simple present tense.

   _____

   _____

3. Which of the five senses does the writer use to describe this kind of weather? Give examples to support your answer.

_____

_____

4. A good descriptive paragraph uses adjectives that help the reader feel what it is like to be in the situation. List any five adjectives in "Danger from the Sky." Then write the feelings they describe.

Adjective	Feelings
a. _____	_____
b. _____	_____
c. _____	_____
d. _____	_____
e. _____	_____

Descriptive Paragraph 3

The next paragraph describes what the writer's mother did while she worked in her garden. Notice how often the writer appeals to the readers' senses of sight and touch.

Preview Questions

1. What flowers can you name?

2. What is a rose? What does the rose symbolize to you?

3. When you think of a garden, especially a flower garden, what sensory adjectives immediately come to mind?

Example Paragraph 4

My Mother's Special Garden

My father **constantly teased** my mother about the amount of time she spent in her beautiful rose garden. He told her that she treated the garden as if it were a human being, perhaps even her best friend. However, Mom **ignored** his teasing and got up early every morning to take care of her special plants. She would walk among the thick green bushes that were covered with huge flowers of every color. While she was walking, she would **remove** any **weeds** that **threatened** her delicate beauties. She also **trimmed** the old flowers to make room

constantly: always, without stopping

to tease: to make fun of someone or something in a playful or joking manner

to ignore: to not pay attention to someone or something

to remove: to take out quickly

a weed: a useless, unwanted plant

to threaten: to put in danger, promise to harm

to trim: to cut to make something look neat

for their bright replacements. Any unwanted **pests** were quickly killed. When she was finished, she always returned from the garden with a wonderful smile and an armful of **fragrant** flowers for us all to enjoy.

a pest: an unwanted insect

fragrant: pleasant smelling

Post-Reading

1. What does this paragraph describe?

_____

_____

2. Can any sentences be deleted without changing the paragraph's meaning? If yes, which ones, and why? If no, why not?

_____

_____

3. The writer's mother treated the roses as if they were human beings. Find two example sentences from the paragraph that show how she protected her roses.

a. _____

_____

b. _____

_____

Grammar for Writing

Using Adjectives in Writing

Adjectives are important in a descriptive paragraph. They help the reader see the person or thing the writer is describing.

The **tall**, **graceful** bride in her **white** dress walked down the **long** aisle to meet her **proud** groom.

Explanation	Examples
An **adjective** describes a noun and usually answers one or more of the following questions: *Which one?* this, that, these, those *What kind?* big, old, yellow, delicate *How many?* some, few, many, two *How much?* enough, some, less, more	her **white** dress the **long** aisle her **proud** groom
Adjectives come **before** the nouns they describe.	The **angry** customers complained about the **poor** service in the **new** restaurant.
When a sentence has a linking verb, the adjective modifies the subject and comes immediately **after** the verb. Linking verbs: be become seem feel taste sound appear remain keep look	The teacher is **intelligent** and **kind**. The soup tastes **good**. Mr. Currier feels **ill**. The decorations in the café looked **horrible**.
If writers use multiple adjectives to describe a noun, the order is often: Number Observation / opinion Size Shape Age Color Origin Material	the **beautiful old stone** building a **red Italian sports** car a **round green plastic** dish

ACTIVITY 5 Correcting the Location of Descriptive Adjectives

Read each sentence. Circle all the descriptive adjectives. Are the adjectives placed correctly? If the sentence is correct, write C on the line. If you find an adjective error, draw an arrow from the adjective to its correct location in the sentence. Add commas if needed.

1. _____ John's puppy chewed on his shoes (new.)

2. _____ A yellow piece of paper is on the floor.

3. _____ The teacher wrote our assignment on the blackboard old.

4. _____ My best friend wrote a letter long.

5. _____ The five black dogs chased the police car.

6. _____ Colorado is a place great to go skiing when it is cold.

7. _____ My neighbor found a large wallet stuffed with new one-dollar bills.

8. _____ The gourmet chef created a slightly spicy but delicious meal.

9. _____ The clock on the rough cement wall of the busy railway station was antique.

10. _____ Egyptian pyramids are an example excellent of ancient architecture.

11. _____ My brother bought two cotton new sheets on sale yesterday.

12. _____ To make this spaghetti sauce, you need six red juicy tomatoes.

ACTIVITY 6 Adding Adjectives

Read each sentence. Write descriptive adjectives in the blanks. You may write more than one adjective in each blank. Then compare answers with your classmates.

1. The _____tired_____ teacher walked into the _____noisy_____ room.

2. The _____ couple watched a(n) _____ sunset.

3. My _____ coworker is a (n) _____ athlete.

4. The _____ computer sat on a(n) _____ table.

5. That _____ spider scared my _____ sister.

6. The _____ car raced down the _____ road.

7. My _____ feet ached from walking on the _____ sidewalk.

8. Brittany wore a _____ dress to the _____ party last night.

9. The _____ cow ate _____ grass in the _____ field.

10. A _____ boy sat on the _____ ground and played with

some _____ toys.

ACTIVITY 7 **Writing Descriptive Sentences Using Adjectives**

Read each set of nouns. Using the nouns, write an original sentence with at least two adjectives. Circle the adjectives.

1. vacation / California

   People who want the (perfect) vacation should visit (sunny) California.

2. students / computers

   _____

3. dictionaries / libraries

   _____

4. trees / forest

   _____

5. skyscraper / city

   _____

Using Positive and Negative Adjectives for More Precise Meanings

When you write, it is important to use words that have the precise meaning that you want. Many times English has two or more adjectives that have the same basic meaning, but one is positive and the other is negative. Knowing multiple adjectives is important to make your writing more precise.

The **thrifty** old man saved all his money for his retirement. (positive meaning)

The **stingy** old man saved all his money for his retirement. (negative meaning)

Look up *thrifty* and *stingy* in your dictionary. The basic meanings for these words are similar—they both describe someone who is careful with money. However, there is a big difference in the feeling these words give to the reader or listener. The *thrifty* person is wise and economical with money, but the *stingy* person is greedy and does not want to spend or share money.

The next two descriptive paragraphs are about the same topic. Read the paragraphs and underline the adjectives. There are 13 descriptive adjectives in Example Paragraph 5 and 11 descriptive adjectives in Example Paragraph 6. The first adjective in each paragraph has been underlined for you.

Example Paragraph 5

The Blue River is an <u>important</u> part of the forest, and the quality of the river shapes the environment around it. The fresh, clear water is home to a wide variety of fish and plants. Colorful trout compete with other fish for the abundant supply of insects near the beautiful river. The tall trees near the river are green and healthy. Wild deer come to drink the sweet water and rest in the shadows cast on the grassy banks of the river.

Example Paragraph 6

The Blue River is an <u>important</u> part of the forest, and the quality of the river shapes the environment around it. The slow brown water does not contain fish or plants. Small trout struggle with other fish to catch the limited number of insects that live near the dirty river. The old trees near the river are almost leafless. They do not provide adequate protection for the wild animals that come to drink from the polluted river.

1. Briefly, what is being described in each paragraph?

   Example Paragraph 5 _____

   Example Paragraph 6 _____

2. What is your impression of the topic in Example Paragraph 5? What words helped you form this opinion?

   _____

   _____

   _____

   _____

3. What is your impression of the topic in Example Paragraph 6? What words helped you form this opinion?

   _____

   _____

   _____

   _____

4. Can you find an adjective in one paragraph that has the opposite meaning of an adjective in the other paragraph? For example, we can say that *clear* in Example Paragraph 5 is opposite in meaning to *brown* in Example Paragraph 6. Can you find other examples?

   _____

   _____

   _____

   _____

Using Bilingual and English Learner Dictionaries

Bilingual Dictionaries

A bilingual dictionary is very helpful when you are first learning English. However, be careful when you use this kind of dictionary. It is easy to choose the wrong word listed in the entry. In fact, the most common error is to choose the first word that you find. You should always read all of the possible translations to find the best word that accurately fits in your sentence.

English Learner's Dictionaries

An English Learner's Dictionary is helpful for developing your growing writing skills. This kind of dictionary often includes simple definitions, clear sample sentences, and synonyms. It can help you expand your vocabulary and find the correct usage for common, academic, and idiomatic words and expressions. In addition, the definitions are written using high frequency vocabulary, so it is a great opportunity to practice useful English.

ACTIVITY 9 **Writing Positive and Negative Adjectives**

Think of adjectives that can describe the nouns listed below. In the first blank, write one or more **positive** adjectives. In the second blank, write **negative** adjectives.

Remember: The purpose of this activity is to increase your vocabulary, so do not use simple or general words, such as *nice* or *bad*. Use your dictionary to find the precise vocabulary to express your ideas. This will help you increase your writing vocabulary.

Noun	Positive	Negative
1. cheese	creamy, buttery, light	rancid, smelly, stinky
2. rock		
3. painting		
4. laughter		
5. flavor		
6. smell		
7. music		
8. texture		

ACTIVITY 10 **Changing Meaning with Descriptive Adjectives**

The paragraph below describes a man walking into a room. Many of the adjectives have been deleted. Fill in each blank with an adjective and create your own paragraph.

The _____ man entered the _____ room. He had hair. He wore a(n)

_____ suit with _____ shoes. The man was very _____ . Everyone

in the room was _____ when they saw him. He was such a(n) _____ man!

They could not believe that he was in the room with them.

Next, rewrite your paragraph in the space below. Be sure to indent and add an original title. Then switch books with a partner and compare paragraphs. What impression do you have of the man in your partner's paragraph? Is it positive or negative?

_____

_____

_____

_____

_____

_____

_____

_____

_____

Grammar for Writing

Using Prepositions of Location to Describe

To be precise in description, writers often need to indicate where something or someone is, especially in relation to something or someone else. For example, if you are describing a room, you can describe what is on the right side, what is on the left side, what is on the ceiling, and what is on the floor.

When you tell the location of something, it is important to use the correct **preposition of location**, followed by a noun. This noun after a preposition is called the **object of the preposition**. This preposition and noun combination is called a **prepositional phrase** (e.g., *in the kitchen*).

Study these examples (the prepositional phrases are bold).

> The new bank is **on Wilson Road near the park.**

> **On the left**, there is an old sofa. **On the right**, there are two wooden chairs.

> **Next to the river**, there is a grassy field that goes **from Wilson Road to the corner of Maple Street and Lee Road**.

Common Prepositions of Location

above	before	far from	on top of
across	behind	from	opposite
after	below	in	outside
against	beneath	in back of	over
ahead of	beside	in front of	past
along	between	inside	throughout
among	beyond	near	under
around	by	next to	
at	close to	on	

ACTIVITY 11 Using Prepositions of Location to Describe a Place

Write five true sentences about the location of things or people in your classroom. Circle the prepositions and underline the objects of the preposition. The first one has been done for you.

1.   The teacher's desk is (in front of) the whiteboard.

2.

3.

4.

5.

6.

ACTIVITY 12 Studying Example Paragraphs with Prepositions of Location

Discuss the Preview Questions with your classmates. Then read the example paragraphs and answer the questions that follow.

Paragraph with Prepositions of Location 1

The following paragraph describes a room in a house. Notice how often the writer appeals to the reader's sense of sight by describing the location of the things in the room.

Preview Questions

1. What are three things that most people expect to find in a living room?

2. Is your living room always neat? Usually neat? Almost never neat?

3. What is in the middle of your living room? On the left side? On the right side?

Example Paragraph 7

A Great Living Room

My living room may be small, but it is **tidy** and well organized. On the right, there is a wooden bookcase with four shelves. On top of the bookcase is a small lamp with a dark base and a blue lampshade. The first and third shelves are filled with some of my favorite books, including an English-French dictionary. On the second shelf, there is an old clock with **faded** numbers on it that my grandfather gave me when I was young. The bottom shelf has a few picture frames. On the opposite side of the room is a television set with a DVD player and my small movie collection on top of it. Between the television and the bookcase is a large sofa. My cat Lucky is sleeping comfortably on the right side of the sofa. Lying near the other end of the sofa is one of his toys. Directly in front of the sofa, there is a long coffee table with short legs. On the right side of this table are two magazines. Perhaps the most **striking** thing in the room is the beautiful beach painting above the sofa. This beautiful painting shows a peaceful beach scene with a sailboat on the right, far from the beach. Although it is a small room, everything in my living room is in its place.

tidy: neat, clean, arranged, organized

faded: difficult to see

striking: exceptional, very noticeable

Post-Reading

1. Why did the writer write this paragraph?

    _____ **a.** to define a living room

    _____ **b.** to describe a living room

    _____ **c.** to explain the process of creating a good living room

2. What is the sequence of describing the room?

    _____ **a.** from right to left to middle

    _____ **b.** from left to right to middle

    _____ **c.** from right to middle to left

    _____ **d.** from left to middle to right

3. Underline the prepositional phrases. How many are there? Count carefully! _____

4. In the topic sentence, the writer says that the room is tidy. Can you find words or phrases that paint this image for the reader?

    _____

    _____

    _____

5. Can you think of some description to add to one part of the room? Use your imagination to write a sentence for that area of the room. Use prepositions of location.

    _____

    _____

    _____

Paragraph with Prepositions of Location 2

This paragraph describes a famous monument in New York Harbor. Notice how often the writer appeals to the reader's sense of sight by describing different parts of the monument.

Preview Questions

1. If you have visited the Statue of Liberty, what was the experience like? What, if anything, was different from what you expected?

2. How high do you think the Statue of Liberty is? What does the Statue of Liberty symbolize?

3. When you think of the Statue of Liberty, what adjectives come to mind?

Example Paragraph 8

The Statue of Liberty

The Statue of Liberty, an internationally-known **symbol** of freedom that was completed in 1886, is certainly an impressive structure. The statue is of a woman who is wearing long, **flowing** robes. On her head, she has a **crown** of seven **spikes** that represent the seven oceans and the seven continents. The statue weighs 450,000 pounds and is 152 feet high. The statue appears much larger, however, because it stands on a **pedestal** that is about 150 feet high. In her raised right hand, the woman holds a **torch**. In her left hand, she carries a tablet with the date "July 4, 1776" written on the cover. At her feet lie broken chains, which symbolize an escape to freedom. The Statue of Liberty is an amazing monument.

a symbol: a figure, a representation

flowing: moving easily

a crown: a decoration for the head to show high position, often worn by kings and queens

a spike: a point

a pedestal: a base

a torch: an instrument for carrying fire as light

1. What is the writer's purpose for writing this paragraph?

   _____ **a.** to inform the reader of the history of the Statue of Liberty

   _____ **b.** to explain why the Statue of Liberty was built

   _____ **c.** to tell the steps in the construction of the Statue of Liberty

   _____ **d.** to describe the Statue of Liberty

2. What is the sequence of describing the Statue?

   _____ **a.** body — head — base — right hand — left hand — feet

   _____ **b.** body — head — base — left hand — right hand — feet

   _____ **c.** body — right hand — left hand — head — base — feet

   _____ **d.** body — left hand — right hand — head — base — feet

3. The writer organizes the description of parts of the statue by location. To help you understand this organization better, answer these three questions:

   a. Where is the tablet? _____

   b. Is the statue on the ground? If not, what is it on? _____

   c. Where is the torch? _____

Grammar for Writing

Using Correct Word Order with Prepositions of Location

Explanation	Examples
Prepositional phrases of location can occur at the end of a sentence.	A fat, fluffy cat was sleeping **on top of the bookcase**.
Prepositional phrases of location can also occur at the beginning of a sentence. Use a comma between the prepositional phrase and the rest of the sentence.	**On top of the bookcase,** a fat, fluffy cat was sleeping.
If you want to move a prepositional phrase of location to the beginning of a sentence with the verb *be*, you must **invert the subject and the verb and drop the comma** after the prepositional phrase. This word order is more common in writing than in speaking.	✓ An empty pizza box [subject] was [verb] **under the sofa**. ✓ **Under the sofa** was [verb] an empty pizza box [subject]. (No comma) ✗ **Under the sofa,** an empty pizza box was.

Read the paragraph. Circle the 20 prepositions. Underline the object of each preposition (the noun after each preposition). Then correct the two comma errors.

Example Paragraph 9

Gandhi

Although I have read about hundreds of famous people, one of the most interesting people in this group is Mahatma Gandhi of India. Gandhi was a great man who helped India win independence from Great Britain. He is most known for his peaceful methods during this important struggle, and his actions began other movements for equal rights all over the world. Gandhi was born, in 1869. This great hero's real name was Mohandas Karamchand Gandhi, but many people know him simply as Mahatma Gandhi. The title "Mahatma" means "Great Soul" and was given to him, in 1914 because he did so many good things for so many people. Unfortunately, Gandhi's life ended in 1948 when he was killed by a shooter. When I read about this great person, I realize how little I actually know about his life, and I am very eager for more information about him.

Building Better Vocabulary

ACTIVITY 14 **Word Associations**

Circle the word or phrase that is most closely related to the word or phrase on the left. If necessary, use a dictionary to check the meaning of words you do not know.

	A	B
1. eager for X to happen	you don't want X to happen	you want X to happen
2. delicate	can break easily	will never break
3. to recall	to remember	to understand
4. a skyscraper	high	low
5. an assault	an attack	an origin
6. to descend	10, 11, 12, 13	13, 12, 11, 10
7. to rip	to send	to tear
8. a pedestal	a statue	a person
9. constantly	always	never
10. a syrup	a liquid	a solid
11. to argue with a person	discuss something great	discuss something bad
12. to tease	to make fun of	to try to understand
13. precise	approximate	exact
14. a crown	your feet	your head
15. to roar	loud	soft

ACTIVITY 15 **Using Collocations**

Fill in each blank with the word on the left that most naturally completes the phrase on the right. If necessary, use a dictionary to check the meaning of words you do not know.

1. storm / worker   a skilled _____

2. of / to   a symbol _____ freedom

3. life / world   all over the _____

4. bank / body   a slender _____

5. come / go   to _____ to mind

6. fish / photo   a faded _____

7. peaceful / principal   the _____ reason

8. dress / office   a tidy _____

9. flowers / human beings fragrant _____

10. of / with   stuffed _____ feathers

11. broken / written   _____ chains

12. common / popular   a very _____ error

Original Student Writing: Descriptive Paragraph

ACTIVITY 16 **Original Writing Practice**

Write a paragraph that describes something. Your goal is to give the reader an impression of what you are describing. Follow these guidelines:

- Choose a topic such as a favorite childhood memory or a famous monument.
- Brainstorm some sensory adjectives (sight, hearing, smell, taste, and touch).
- Write a topic sentence with a controlling idea.
- Write supporting sentences that relate to the topic.
- Make sure the adjectives mean precisely what you want them to mean—check both the positive and negative meanings.
- Use prepositional phrases of location in your paragraph. Put some at the beginning of sentences and some at the end of sentences because sentence variety is important to good writing.
- Make sure your concluding sentence restates the topic.
- Use at least two of the vocabulary words or phrases presented in Activity 14 and Activity 15. Underline these words and phrases in your paragraph.

If you need ideas for words and phrases, see the Useful Vocabulary for Better Writing on pages 118–122.

ACTIVITY 17 Peer Editing

Exchange papers from Activity 16 with a partner. Read your partner's paragraph. Then use Peer Editing Sheet 1 on ELTNGL.com/sites/els to help you comment on your partner's paragraph. Be sure to offer positive suggestions and comments that will help your partner improve his or her writing. Consider your partner's comments as you revise your own paragraph.

Additional Topics for Writing

Here are some ideas for descriptive paragraphs. When you write, follow the guidelines in Activity 16.

PHOTO
TOPIC: Look at the photo on pages 22–23. Describe a national monument that is important to you. What does it look like? What feelings does the monument inspire in you?

TOPIC 2: Describe a family tradition. When do you follow the tradition? Why is the tradition important to you and your family?

TOPIC 3: Describe your favorite or least favorite meal. Be sure to tell how the food tastes, smells, and looks.

TOPIC 4: Describe something that makes you happy, sad, nervous, or afraid.

TOPIC 5: Describe a person you know. What is this person like? What are some of his or her characteristics? Make sure that the description would allow your reader to identify the person in a crowd.

Timed Writing

How quickly can you write in English? There are many times when you must write quickly, such as on a test. It is important to feel comfortable during those times. Timed-writing practice can make you feel better about writing quickly in English.

1. Take out a piece of paper.

2. Read the writing prompt.

3. Brainstorm ideas for five minutes.

4. Write a short paragraph (six to ten sentences).

5. You have 25 minutes to write.

In your opinion, what is the ideal teacher? Describe your ideal teacher. Which characteristics make this kind of teacher ideal to you? (Do not use names of current teachers, but you should use their characteristics that you consider ideal.)

NOTES

CONNECTED LIVES 3

Participants attend an online gaming festival in Leipzig, Germany.

EXPLORE THE THEME

A Look at the information on these pages and answer the questions.

1. According to Alexa.com, what are the most visited websites in the world? Which are more popular: social media sites or search engines?

2. Which of these websites do you visit regularly? Can you think of other popular websites that aren't on the list?

B Match the correct form of the words and phrases in blue to their definitions.

_____ (n) the act of looking carefully for something

_____ (v) to start or put into operation

_____ (v) to connect to a computer system by typing a particular set of letters or numbers

People in Hong Kong connect with their neighbors and their city while playing Pokémon GO.

THE WORLD'S TOP 10 WEBSITES

How often do you **log in** to Facebook? Is there a website that you check every day? Alexa.com tracks millions of Internet users and compiles lists of the most visited websites. Here are its 2017 rankings of the top 10 websites worldwide.

Unsurprisingly, the world's most popular website is Google. This indicates that the majority of Internet use is driven by the **search** for information. YouTube and Facebook are the next most popular, followed by Baidu (in 4th place). **Launched** in 2000, Baidu is the leading Chinese-language search engine. The Indian version of Google also makes the list (in 8th place).

		Time spent[1]	Pages viewed[2]	Linked sites[3]
1	Google.com	8:34	8.30	2,670,033
2	YouTube.com	9:10	5.30	2,097,022
3	Facebook.com	11:50	4.52	6,442,560
4	Baidu.com	7:56	6.54	96,538
5	Wikipedia.org	4:22	3.30	1,131,376
6	Yahoo.com	4:23	3.80	457,873
7	Reddit.com	15:51	10.38	371,615
8	Google.co.in	8:10	7.05	20,426
9	QQ.com	4:58	4.39	177,323
10	Twitter.com	6:27	3.46	4,494,842

[1] Daily time spent on site (in minutes) per visitor
[2] Daily page views per visitor
[3] Total number of sites that link to this site

Reading 1

PREPARING TO READ

A The words in **blue** below are used in the reading passage on pages 53–54. Complete each sentence with the correct word. Use a dictionary to help you.

collaborate	potential	feature	contribution
investigate	participant	accurate	

1. A(n) _____ is a person who takes part in something.

2. When you _____ something, you try to find out what happened or what the truth is.

3. _____ information and statistics are correct to a very detailed level.

4. To _____ means to work together on an activity or project to achieve a common goal.

5. If you make a(n) _____ to something, you help make it successful.

6. Something with _____ has the necessary abilities or qualities to become successful in the future.

7. A(n) _____ of something is an important aspect of it.

B Discuss these questions with a partner.
1. How often do you **log in** to social media sites? Which is your favorite one?
2. What **contributions** has social media made to society? Can you think of any specific examples?

C Brainstorm a list of reasons you or people you know have used the Internet to collaborate. Discuss with a partner and note your ideas.

_____

_____

D Look at the title and the subheads of the reading passage on pages 53–54. Then skim the first paragraph. What do you think the reading passage is mainly about? Check your answer as you read.

a. the different ways archaeologists can collaborate with one another over the Internet
b. how the Internet is changing the field of archaeology
c. how the Internet contributed to a major archaeological discovery

THE POWER OF CROWDS

🎧 Track 3

A   Every day, people use the Internet to **collaborate** and share information. Today, scientists and archaeologists[1] are using the power of the Internet to **investigate** the past in a new, exciting way. The approach is known as crowdsourcing, and it involves asking the public for help with a project. Crowdsourcing has the **potential** to completely change modern archaeology.

SOLVING A MYSTERY

B   Scientists in the United States and Mongolia used the Internet to try to solve an 800-year-old mystery: the location of Genghis Khan's tomb. Genghis Khan was the founder of the Mongol Empire, one of the largest empires in history. When he died in 1227, he was buried in an unmarked grave.

C   Experts believe that Genghis Khan's final resting place is somewhere near the Burkhan Khaldun, a sacred[2] Mongolian mountain. It's a difficult place to get to and covers a huge area, so the scientists had to rely on satellite[3] images. However, there were over 85,000 images to study, so they needed a lot of help.

[1] An **archaeologist** is a person who studies human history by digging up items buried underground.
[2] Something that is **sacred** is believed to have a special religious purpose or meaning.
[3] A **satellite** is a device that is sent into space to collect information, to capture images, or to be part of a communications system.

More than 10,000 volunteers or "citizen scientists" joined the **search**. They **logged in** to a website and labeled landmarks[4] on very detailed satellite images of the area. The landmarks could be roads, rivers, modern structures, or ancient structures. **Participants** also labeled anything else that looked unusual.

According to project leader Albert Lin, humans can often do this kind of work better than computers. "What a computer can't do is look for 'weird things,'" he says. Lin's team used the information from the volunteers to decide on the best places to visit and study. The project has identified more than 50 sites that might be related to Genghis Khan's tomb. The exact location is still unknown, but Lin believes that we are getting closer to finding out this great secret.

PROTECTING TREASURES

Crowdsourcing is also being used by National Geographic Explorer and archaeologist Dr. Sarah Parcak. In 2017, Parcak **launched** GlobalXplorer, a citizen science project that aims to find and protect important archaeological sites using satellite images. In particular, it protects sites from looters—people who steal ancient objects and sell them. "If we don't go and find these sites," says Parcak, "looters will." Looting pits are easy to spot in satellite images, so participants can look for signs of looting and illegal construction. The project launched in Peru, which has large numbers of historical sites from many different cultures.

GlobalXplorer is designed like a game. Participants first watch online videos that teach them how to identify certain **features** on satellite images. Then they study and flag[5] satellite images on their own. They look at more than 250,000 square kilometers of land, broken into 100 × 100 meter "tiles." Since the participants don't have professional experience, a certain number of them have to agree on the results before the data is considered useful. Once enough volunteers say that they see the same thing, Parcak and her team will check for themselves before passing the information along to archaeologists on the ground. The "players" receive a score based on how **accurate** they are.

"Most people don't get to make scientific **contributions** or discoveries in their everyday lives," Parcak says. "But we're all born explorers … We want to find out more about other people, and about ourselves and our past." Now, thanks to crowdsourcing projects like GlobalXplorer, anyone with a computer and an Internet connection can be part of a new age of discovery.

[4] A **landmark** is a building or other place (e.g., a large tree or a statue) that is easily noticed and recognized.
[5] When you **flag** something, you mark it for attention.

Archaeologist Sarah Parcak examines a satellite image.

UNDERSTANDING THE READING

A According to the reading passage, the Internet is enabling collaboration through crowdsourcing. How does this work?

UNDERSTANDING THE MAIN IDEA

   a. A small group of people connected to the Internet work together on a project.

   b. A large group of people connected to the Internet contribute toward a shared goal.

B Complete the chart below using information from the reading passage.

IDENTIFYING DETAILS

Lin's Project	Parcak's Project
studies an area in the country of 1 _____	studies sites in the country of 4 _____
aims to find the tomb of 2 _____	aims to protect sites from 5 _____
Participants look at satellite images and label landmarks and other 3 _____ features.	Participants look at satellite images and flag any signs of looting and 6 _____ .

> **CRITICAL THINKING** You **make inferences** when you make logical guesses about things a writer does not say directly. This is also called "reading between the lines."

C Work with a partner. What can you infer from each statement from the reading passage? Circle the correct inference.

CRITICAL THINKING: MAKING INFERENCES

1. *More than 10,000 volunteers or "citizen scientists" joined the search.*
   a. A lot of people don't know much about Genghis Khan.
   b. A lot of people are interested in finding Genghis Khan's tomb.

2. *[GlobalXplorer] protects sites from looters—people who steal ancient objects and sell them.*
   a. Many people don't appreciate the true value of ancient objects.
   b. Ancient objects are worth a lot of money.

3. *The project launched in Peru, which has large numbers of historical sites from many different cultures.*
   a. Because of its rich history, Peru is an ideal place to start the project.
   b. Peruvians are very proud of their country's rich and diverse history.

D Would you prefer to join Lin's project or Parcak's project? Discuss with a partner and give reasons for your choice.

CRITICAL THINKING: REFLECTING

DEVELOPING READING SKILLS

Taking notes on a reading passage has two main benefits. First, it helps you understand the information better. It also helps you organize important information for writing assignments and for tests.

It is often helpful to use some kind of graphic organizer when you take notes. Use graphic organizers that best match the type of passage you are reading. Many reading passages are a mixture of text types, so you may want to use more than one graphic organizer:

- **T-chart:** problem-solution, cause-effect, pros-cons, two sides of a topic (see page 55)
- **mind map** (or **concept map** or **word web**): description, classification
- **Venn diagram:** comparison of similarities and differences
- **traditional outline:** any type
- **flow chart** or **timeline:** process or events over time (see below and page 62)

UNDERSTANDING A PROCESS

A Read the information about how GlobalXplorer works. As you read, underline the different steps in the process.

GlobalXplorer is designed like a game. Participants first watch online videos that teach them how to identify certain features on satellite images. Then they study and flag satellite images on their own. They look at more than 250,000 square kilometers of land, broken into 100 × 100 meter "tiles." Since the participants don't have professional experience, a certain number of them have to agree on the results before the data is considered useful. Once enough volunteers say that they see the same thing, Parcak and her team will check for themselves before passing the information along to archaeologists on the ground. The "players" receive a score based on how accurate they are.

TAKING NOTES

B Complete the flow chart using the information above. Then compare answers with a partner.

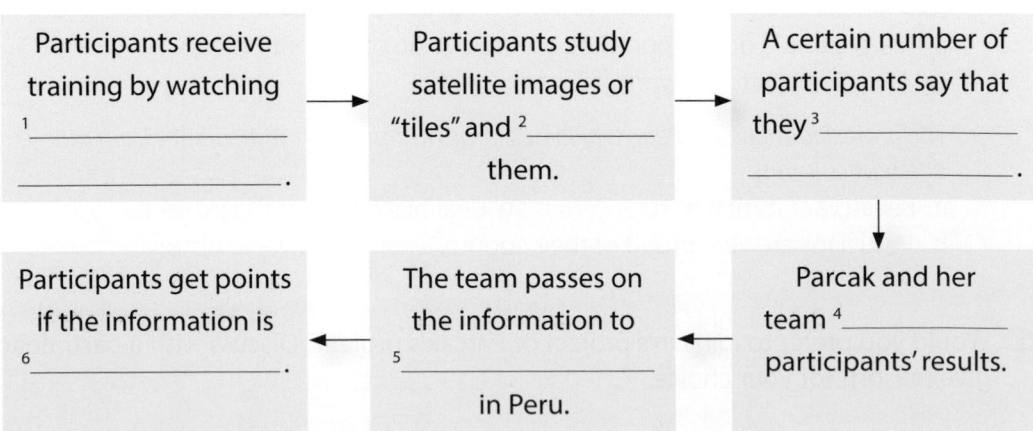

Participants receive training by watching 1_____. → Participants study satellite images or "tiles" and 2_____ them. → A certain number of participants say that they 3_____.

Participants get points if the information is 6_____. ← The team passes on the information to 5_____ in Peru. ← Parcak and her team 4_____ participants' results.

Video

Albert Lin rides out to explore a site in Mongolia.

CITIZEN SCIENTISTS

BEFORE VIEWING

A Why do you think people are interested in finding Genghis Khan's tomb? Discuss your ideas with a partner.

BRAINSTORMING

B Read the information about Genghis Khan. Then answer the questions.

LEARNING ABOUT THE TOPIC

Genghis Khan was one of the most feared leaders of all time. Born around 1160, he was originally named "Temujin." At the age of 20, he began building a large army to bring all the people of Mongolia under his rule. As leader of the Mongol Empire, he introduced a new alphabet and a new type of money. He also devised a system of laws and regulations, and allowed freedom of religion—long before that idea spread to other parts of the world. At the same time, however, he launched violent military campaigns against his enemies. After his death, the Mongol Empire grew to become one of the largest of all time. It stretched east to west from the Sea of Japan to Eastern Europe, and north to south from Siberia to Southeast Asia. Today, Genghis Khan is still regarded as one of the most influential people in history.

1. Why is Genghis Khan one of the most feared leaders of all time?

    _____

2. List two ways Genghis Khan's empire set a model for modern society.

    a. _____

    b. _____

C Below are some quotes from the video. Match the correct form of each **bold** word or phrase to its definition.

> "Citizen scientists around the world scan the images and **tag** anything that looks unusual."
>
> "These are the most recent tags that have been **uploaded** onto the data pads."
>
> "We're going to scan every single one of the human computation sites that have been picked out on that mountain and try to **figure out** what people saw."

1. _____ (v) to mark or attach a label to

2. _____ (v) to investigate or think something through in order to understand it

3. _____ (v) to transfer data from one computer to a central computer or the Internet

WHILE VIEWING

A ▶ Watch the video. Choose the best alternative title for it.

a. How Crowdsourcing Led Us to an Ancient Tomb
b. Journeying on Horseback Across the Burkhan Khaldun
c. Lessons from a Crowdsourcing Failure

B ▶ Watch the video again and answer the questions below.

1. What is a good indicator that something is man-made?

_____

2. How does the team know that this is not Genghis Khan's tomb?

_____

3. Why is Lin encouraged by the discovery of this tomb?

_____

AFTER VIEWING

A Work with a partner. If you were able to interview Albert Lin, what questions would you ask him?

_____

_____

B Below is an excerpt from the reading passage on page 54:

According to project leader Albert Lin, humans can often do this kind of work better than computers. "What a computer can't do is look for 'weird things,'" he says.

What do you think Lin means by this? Discuss with a partner and include an example from the video to support your answer.

Reading 2

PREPARING TO READ

A The words in **blue** below are used in the reading passage on pages 60–61. Read their definitions and then complete each sentence with the correct word.

BUILDING VOCABULARY

A **tribe** is a group of people who live in the same place and share a common culture.

Voting is the activity of choosing someone or something in an election.

If something exists in the **virtual** world, it exists only on computers or on the Internet.

Remote areas are far away from cities and places where most people live.

An **environmentally** responsible person is concerned with the protection of the natural world of land, sea, air, plants, and animals.

When you **advertise** a product, you provide information about it so that more people know about the product.

A **tool** can refer to anything you use for a particular task or purpose.

If something is **global**, it affects all parts of the world.

1. A lot of companies _____ their products on TV and online.

2. Many companies these days are trying to be more _____ friendly. For example, some automobile companies are producing more electric cars.

3. The Internet is a useful _____ for communication.

4. Some online games have _____ cities. These places aren't real; they only exist online.

5. In most democracies, people choose their leaders by _____ for them.

6. There are still some _____ areas in the developing world that don't have Internet access.

7. Most social media sites are _____—people from all over the world can use them.

8. In traditional Fijian society, each _____ has its own chief or leader.

B Discuss these questions with a partner.

USING VOCABULARY

1. What is the most **remote** place you have been to? Did you like it there?
2. Do you generally prefer **virtual** or face-to-face communication? What are the advantages (pros) and disadvantages (cons) of each?

C Skim the reading passage on pages 60–61. Why do you think it is titled "Internet Island"? Note your ideas below. Then check your ideas as you read the passage.

PREDICTING

_____

INTERNET ISLAND

Ben Keene (right) with members of his tribe

THE IDEA

On January 14, 2006, Ben Keene received an email that changed his life. It was from his friend Mark James. The subject line read: "A TRIBE IS WANTED." Keene and James, both 26, had wanted to create an Internet start-up.[1] Here was James's new idea: We will create an online community and call it a tribe. We will make decisions about rules through discussions and online voting. Then we will do something that no one has ever done—our virtual tribe will become a real one. We will travel to a remote island and form a partnership with a local tribe. We will build an environmentally friendly community and share it with the world.

James got this idea from social networking websites. He noticed that people spent a lot of time on these sites, but they spent most of their time posting messages and sharing music. In James's view, these sites could be used for so much more.

THE ISLAND

Keene liked the idea, and he and James named their website Tribewanted.com. Then they began looking for an island for their tribe. Around the same time, Tui Mali—the chief of a tribe in Fiji—wanted to find someone to develop his small island called Vorovoro. Although the main islands of Fiji were becoming very modern, Vorovoro was not. A few people on Vorovoro had cell phones or worked on one of the main islands, but most lived in very small, simple homes with no electricity or running water.

Tui Mali advertised his island on the Internet, and a few weeks later, Keene and James contacted him. They agreed to pay $53,000 for a three-year lease[2] of the island and $26,500 in donations[3] to the community. They also promised jobs for the local tribe members. "We are all excited about Tribewanted," Tui Mali told a local newspaper reporter. "It will provide us with work for the next three years." Tui Mali was happy to have the money, but he also trusted that Keene and James would respect his culture.

THE NEW TRIBE

The Internet tribe attracted people quickly. In a few months, it had 920 members from 25 countries. In September of 2006, Keene and 13 of his tribe members, aged 17 to 59, traveled to the island for the first time. James, meanwhile, stayed at home to manage the website. When Keene's group arrived, the local tribe and Tui Mali were there to greet them.

For several weeks after the newcomers arrived, they worked with the local tribe members. They built buildings, planted crops behind the village, set up clean sources of energy such as solar power, and ate fresh fish from the ocean. As the new and old tribes worked together, they became friends. Eventually, they became one tribe.

Tribewanted brought together groups of people from very different cultures—both on the island and online. Keene and Tui Mali believe the new tribal connections will help Vorovoro develop in a positive way. They hope the island will become more modern without losing its traditional culture.

THE TRIBE KEEPS GROWING

Today, Tribewanted continues to use social networking as a tool to connect in a real environment. Anyone can go to the website to join the online tribe, donate money, or plan a visit. Since Vorovoro, Keene and James have created other tribes in Sierra Leone, Papua New Guinea, Bali, and Italy. They hope to create more communities around the world, bringing people and cultures together in a global Internet tribe.

[1] An Internet start-up is a newly created online business.
[2] A lease is a contract allowing the use of a building or piece of land.
[3] Donations are sums of money or items that someone gives to an organization.

UNDERSTANDING THE READING

UNDERSTANDING
MAIN IDEAS

A The statement in **bold** below is an introductory sentence for a brief summary of the reading passage. Complete the summary by choosing three sentences (a–e) that best express the main ideas of the reading passage.

Ben Keene and Mark James created Tribewanted.com, a virtual community that became a real community.

☐ a. They contacted Tui Mali, the leader of a tribe in Fiji who wanted to modernize his island.

☐ b. Members of the website traveled to the island to help develop it, forming new tribal connections with the local community.

☐ c. James did not go to the island; he had to stay at home to manage the website.

☐ d. Each month, one member of Tribewanted was elected co-chief of the island and served alongside Tui Mali.

☐ e. Keene and James have created new tribes in other places around the world and hope to form a global Internet community.

IDENTIFYING
DETAILS

B Find details in the reading passage to complete each sentence. The sentences are in random order.

1. James and Keene found a small island for their tribe called _____.

2. In September _____, Keene went to the island with 13 other people.

3. James and Keene paid Tui Mali _____ to lease the island for three years.

4. James and Keene named their website _____.

5. Mark James sent a(n) _____ to his friend Ben Keene about starting a tribe.

6. James and Keene started tribes in other places like _____ in Indonesia.

7. The newcomers worked with the _____ people to develop the island. In the end, both groups became one tribe.

SEQUENCING

C Complete the timeline using the sentences in exercise B (1–7).

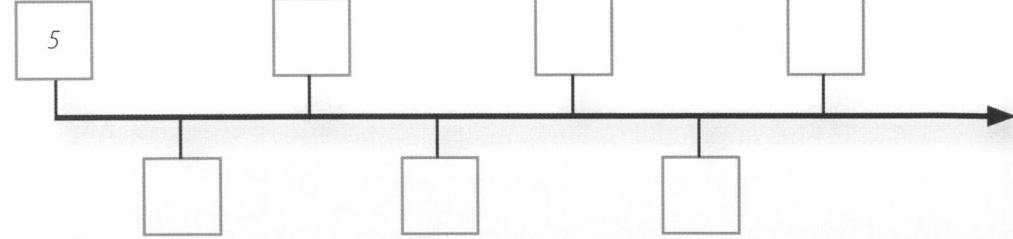

CRITICAL THINKING:
MAKING
INFERENCES

D Discuss these questions with a partner.

1. What kind of people do you think join Tribewanted?

2. How do you think Tribewanted has changed Tui Mali and his tribe members?

Writing

EXPLORING WRITTEN ENGLISH

A Read the sentences (1–5). Then answer the question below.

1. The project <u>has identified</u> over 50 sites that might be related to Genghis Khan's tomb.

2. Lin and Parcak <u>have used</u> citizen scientists to help them find important sites.

3. Parcak's work <u>has helped</u> to protect sites from looters.

4. Since Vorovoro, Keene and James <u>have created</u> new tribes in other countries.

5. Thousands of people <u>have joined</u> Tribewanted in the past few years.

Which of the following statements is true about the actions described by the underlined verbs?

a. The action started and ended in the past.
b. The action started in the past and continues in the present.

LANGUAGE FOR WRITING Using the Present Perfect Tense

We use the present perfect tense:

- for something that began in the past and continues to the present.
- for something that happened at an unspecified time in the past.
- when the time in the past is not important.

To form the present perfect tense, use *have* or *has* and the past participle of a main verb.

*Tui Mali **has lived** in Fiji all his life.*

*We **have advertised** the product on several different social media sites recently.*

*I think the Internet **has improved** our lives in many ways.*

We often use a phrase with *since* to show when something started in the past.

*She **has posted** over 100 photos on Instagram <u>since last month</u>.*

An aerial view
of Vorovoro

B Complete the sentences using the present perfect tense of the verbs in parentheses.

1. Facebook _____ (*make*) it easier for me to keep in touch with my former classmates.

2. Social media sites _____ (*change*) a lot since they first became popular.

3. I _____ (*meet*) a lot of great people through social networking sites.

4. Citizen scientists _____ (*contribute*) to many important research projects in the past few years.

5. GlobalXplorer _____ (*form*) a partnership with the Sustainable Preservation Initiative (SPI).

6. Since the success of Vorovoro, Tribewanted _____ (*expand*) into Africa and Europe.

C Write three sentences using the present perfect tense. Write about the impact that the Internet has had on your life, and ways that you have used the Internet.

1. _____

_____

2. _____

_____

3. _____

_____

WRITING SKILL Writing a Concluding Sentence

Formal paragraphs often have concluding sentences. A concluding sentence is the last sentence of a paragraph. It ties the paragraph together.

Concluding sentences can state an opinion (either the author's, or a person mentioned in the paragraph), make a prediction, or ask a question for the reader to think about. They can also restate—or summarize—the main idea of a long or complex paragraph. Here are some examples:

I believe that one of the most important skills we can learn is collaboration.
[states an opinion]

GlobalXplorer will help prevent looting of archaeological sites in Peru.
[makes a prediction]

Which crowdsourcing project would you prefer to join?
[asks a question]

In short, the Internet has transformed the field of archaeology.
[restates the main idea]

D Find and underline these concluding sentences from paragraphs earlier in this unit. What does each sentence do? Write **P** (makes a prediction), **O** (gives an opinion), or **R** (restates the main idea).

_____ 1. *Today, Genghis Khan is still regarded as one of the most influential people in history.* (page 57)

_____ 2. *We will build an environmentally friendly community and share it with the world.* (page 61)

_____ 3. *In James's view, these sites could be used for so much more.* (page 61)

E Write a concluding sentence for each paragraph below.

Everywhere you look these days, people are on their phones, tablets, or computers. Some are talking, some are texting, and some are surfing the Web. It seems like people communicate with each other more on social networks and by text than they do in person. According to Tom Rath and Jim Harter, authors of *Wellbeing: The Five Essential Elements*, people should spend up to six hours a day socializing with friends and family in order to increase happiness. Socializing online probably doesn't have the same effect that socializing in person does.

1. [Write a prediction.] _____

   _____

   _____

In my opinion, reading the news online is better than reading a newspaper or watching the news on TV. One reason for this is that readers can comment on articles that they read online. They can have conversations with other readers, and sometimes even with the writer. Also, online articles provide links to additional information. For example, if an article mentions a name, the name is often linked to another article with more information about that person. Finally, online news articles can be easily updated if something changes during the day. For example, an online news site might post an article about a dangerous storm in the morning. If more information about the storm becomes available later that day, it can be added to the article.

2. [Restate the main idea.] _____

   _____

   _____

WRITING TASK

> **GOAL** You are going to write a paragraph on the following topic:
>
> Describe a crowdsourcing project that you know well. Do some research if necessary. Choose one of the following or your own idea:
>
> EyeWire   Galaxy Zoo   Wild Me   iNaturalist   WildScan

TAKING NOTES **A** Look up the crowdsourcing projects above—or other crowdsourcing projects you know about—online. Choose one project and take notes as you read about it.

_____

_____

_____

PLANNING **B** Follow these steps to make notes for your paragraph.

Step 1 Write a topic sentence in the outline below introducing the crowdsourcing project you chose.

Step 2 Complete the outline with details for each question. Don't worry about grammar or spelling. Don't write complete sentences.

Step 3 Write a concluding sentence for your paragraph.

OUTLINE

Topic: What is one way that people have collaborated on the Internet?

Topic Sentence: _____

_____

What is the purpose of the project? _____

_____

How does it work? _____

_____

What has it accomplished so far? _____

_____

Concluding Sentence: _____

_____

FIRST DRAFT **C** Use the information in your outline to write a first draft of your paragraph.

REVISING PRACTICE

The drafts below are similar to the one you are going to write. They are on the topic of Tribewanted.

What did the writer do in Draft 2 to improve the paragraph? Match the changes (a–d) to the highlighted parts.

a. deleted unrelated information
b. corrected a verb form
c. added a concluding sentence
d. added details to explain an idea

Draft 1

Members of Tribewanted.com has collaborated to create virtual and real-life communities all over the world. The founders of the website are Ben Keene and Mark James. They have been friends for a long time. In 2006, James came up with the idea to launch a website to get members to meet and work together to help a community in need. Keene and James learned about a project to help develop an island in Fiji. By this time, many people had signed up online to join the website. Keene and a few members went to the island and worked with the local people there. Together, they accomplished a lot. Tribewanted has since expanded into other areas like Sierra Leone and Papua New Guinea.

Draft 2

Members of Tribewanted.com have collaborated to create virtual and real-life communities all over the world. The founders of the website are Ben Keene and Mark James. In 2006, James came up with the idea to launch a website to get members to meet and work together to help a community in need. Keene and James learned about a project to help develop an island in Fiji. By this time, many people had signed up online to join the website. Keene and a few members went to the island and worked with the local people there. Together, they accomplished a lot. For example, they planted crops and set up environmentally friendly power sources on the island. Tribewanted has since expanded into other areas like Sierra Leone and Papua New Guinea. The website has successfully brought together people from very different cultures to form a real-world tribe.

D Now use the questions below to revise your paragraph.   REVISED DRAFT

- ☐ Does a strong topic sentence introduce the main idea?
- ☐ Does the paragraph include enough details for each supporting idea?
- ☐ Are all verb forms correct?
- ☐ Is there any information that doesn't belong?
- ☐ Does the paragraph have a concluding statement or question?

EDITING PRACTICE

Read the information below.

In sentences using the present perfect tense, remember to:
- use the correct form of *have*.
- use the correct form of the past participle of the main verb. (Be careful with irregular past participles, such as *be—been, do—done, have—had, see—seen,* and *take—taken.*)

Correct one mistake with the present perfect tense in each sentence below.

1. The Internet been in existence for several decades now, but we are still discovering creative ways to use it.

2. Now that it's so easy to share videos, millions of people has posted videos online.

3. Even though I have saw that video a few times, I still find it very funny.

4. Social networks like Facebook and Twitter has changed the way we get our news.

5. The Internet has allow people to share information and collaborate on projects.

6. Sarah Parcak has spend the last several years using satellite images to identify important archaeological sites.

7. Participants in the Galaxy Zoo project have help scientists discover new types of galaxies (star systems) in our universe.

FINAL DRAFT **E** Follow these steps to write a final draft.

1. Check your revised draft for mistakes with the present perfect tense.

2. Now use the checklist on page 88 to write a final draft. Make any other necessary changes.

UNIT REVIEW

Answer the following questions.

1. Would you prefer to participate in a crowdsourcing project or join Tribewanted? Why?

_____

_____

2. What are two things a concluding sentence can do?

_____

_____

3. Do you remember the meanings of these words? Check (✓) the ones you know. Look back at the unit and review the ones you don't know.

Reading 1:

☐ accurate AWL ☐ collaborate ☐ contribution AWL
☐ feature AWL ☐ investigate AWL ☐ launch
☐ log in ☐ participant AWL ☐ potential AWL
☐ search

Reading 2:

☐ advertise ☐ environmentally AWL ☐ global AWL
☐ remote ☐ tool ☐ tribe
☐ virtual AWL ☐ voting

SAVING OUR SEAS

4

A shipwreck attracts a school
of smallmouth grunt fish.

THINK AND DISCUSS

1   Which ocean or sea is nearest your home?
    When was the last time you saw it?

2   Do you eat seafood? If so, what types do you
    eat? If not, why not?

A Look at the information on these pages and answer the questions.

1. What does the map show? What do the colors indicate?
2. How is pollution affecting the four places described? What other problems are mentioned?

B Match the words in yellow to their definitions.

_____ (adj) concerned with earning money

_____ (v) to continue to live in spite of danger

_____ (n) a group of animals or plants whose members share common characteristics

OCEAN IMPACT

Human activities are affecting all of the world's oceans in some way. These activities include fishing, manufacturing, and offshore oil and gas drilling.

Impact of human activity

- ■ Very high
- ■ High
- ■ Medium high
- □ Medium
- ■ Low
- ■ Very low

NORTH AMERICA

NORTH PACIFIC OCEAN

EUROPE

NORTH ATLANTIC OCEAN

AFRICA

EQUATOR

SOUTH AMERICA

SOUTH PACIFIC OCEAN

SOUTH ATLANTIC OCEAN

ANTARCTICA

CARIBBEAN SEA

Pollution and overfishing are causing some fish species to disappear. Due to global warming, the temperature of the water is increasing, too. The rising water temperature makes it more difficult for fish to breathe, swim, and find food.

▶ **Garbage washes ashore on the southern edge of Aruba in the Caribbean.**

NORTH SEA

Pollution from shipping and offshore drilling is causing "dead zones"—places without enough oxygen for plants and fish to survive. Overfishing adds to the problem.

◀ Pollution from offshore oil and gas drilling is one cause of the North Sea's dead zones.

EAST CHINA SEA

Several large rivers bring pollution into the sea. It is also a major commercial fishing area and shipping route. Together, these factors cause serious problems for the ocean environment.

◀ Container ships are a common sight on the rivers that flow into the East China Sea.

ASIA

NORTH PACIFIC OCEAN

EQUATOR

INDIAN OCEAN

AUSTRALIA

CORAL SEA

The sea absorbs the carbon dioxide produced from human activities. As carbon dioxide in the ocean increases, the water becomes more acidic.[1] Plants, fish, and corals cannot survive in acidic water.

◀ The humphead wrasse is among thousands of fish species living in Australia's Coral Sea.

▲ (Main Photo) Waves of sand cover the ocean floor of Australia's Coral Sea.

[1] If something is **acidic**, it has a pH of less than 7. Very strong acids are able to burn holes in things.

Reading 1

PREPARING TO READ

BUILDING VOCABULARY

A The words in **blue** below are used in the reading passage on pages 73–74. Complete each sentence with the correct word. Use a dictionary to help you.

diverse	estimate	doubled	quantity
reduce	restore	stable	

1. If you _____ something, you make it less.

2. If you _____ something, you make it the way it was before.

3. When you _____ a size or number, you make a guess based on the information available.

4. A(n) _____ environment is made up of things that are very different from one another.

5. Something that is _____ is not likely to change.

6. A(n) _____ is an amount of something that can be counted or measured.

7. If something has _____ in size, it has become twice as much or as many.

USING VOCABULARY

B Discuss these questions with a partner.

1. What do fish need to **survive**? What do humans need to survive?

2. Apart from **species** of fish, what other animal species can we find in the ocean?

3. How can we **reduce** pollution?

PREDICTING

C Skim the reading passage on pages 73–74. Check (✓) the topics that you think the reading passage covers. Then check your answers as you read.

☐ 1. why there are fewer big fish in our oceans

☐ 2. why fish migrate

☐ 3. the growth of the fishing industry

☐ 4. the areas that are most affected by overfishing

☐ 5. the causes and effects of ocean pollution

☐ 6. how to protect and restore ocean life

WHERE HAVE ALL THE FISH GONE?

🎧 Track 5

A Throughout history, people have thought of the ocean as a **diverse** and limitless source of food. Today, however, there are clear signs that the oceans do have a limit. Most of the big fish in our oceans—including many of the fish we love to eat—are now gone. One major factor is overfishing. People are taking so many fish from the sea that **species** cannot reproduce[1] quickly enough to maintain their populations. How did this problem start? And what is the future for fish?

SOURCE OF THE PROBLEM

B For centuries, local fishermen caught only enough fish to feed their families and their communities. They used traditional gear like spears and hooks that targeted a single fish at a time. However, in the mid-20th century, more people around the world became interested in fish as a source of protein and healthy fats. In response to this, governments gave money and other help to the fishing industry.

As a result, the fishing industry grew. Large **commercial** fishing companies began catching huge **quantities** of fish. They made a lot of money selling the

[1]When animals **reproduce**, they have babies.

C   fish around the world. In addition, they started using new fishing technologies that made fishing easier. These technologies included sonar[2] to locate fish, and dragging large nets along the ocean floor. Modern equipment enabled commercial fishermen to catch many more fish than local fishermen.

RISE OF THE LITTLE FISH

D   In 2010, the Census of Marine Life **estimated** that 90 percent of the big ocean fish populations are gone, mainly due to overfishing. In particular, commercial fishing has greatly **reduced** the number of large fish such as cod, tuna, and salmon. Today, there are plenty of fish in the sea, but they're mostly just the little ones. Small fish, such as sardines and anchovies, have more than **doubled** in number. This is largely because there aren't enough big fish to eat them.

E   This is a problem because, in order to be **stable**, oceans need predators.[3] Predators are necessary to kill the sick and weak fish. Without them, there are too many unhealthy, small fish in the sea. This can cause serious problems for the sea's food chain and the health of our oceans.

A FUTURE FOR FISH?

F   A study published in 2006 in the journal *Science* made a prediction: If we continue to overfish the oceans, most of the fish that we catch now—from tuna to sardines—will disappear by 2050. However, we can prevent this situation if we **restore** the ocean's biodiversity.[4]

G   Scientists say there are a few ways we can do this. First, commercial fishing companies need to catch fewer large fish. This will increase the number of predator fish in the sea. Another way to improve the biodiversity of the oceans is to develop aquaculture—fish farming. Growing fish on farms means that we catch fewer wild fish. This gives wild fish a chance to **survive** and reproduce. In addition, we can make good choices about what we eat. For example, we can stop eating the fish that are most in danger—like bluefin tuna—or only eat fish from fish farms. If we are careful today, we can still look forward to a future with fish.

▼ **Fish farms, such as this one in Turkey, help protect wild seafood populations.**

[2]**Sonar** technology uses sound waves to locate objects on or under the surface of the water.
[3]**Predators** are animals that kill and eat other animals.
[4]**Biodiversity** is the existence of a wide variety of plant and animal species.

UNDERSTANDING THE READING

A Choose the main idea of each section of the reading passage from the pairs of statements (a or b).

UNDERSTANDING MAIN IDEAS

Source of the Problem
a. Traditional gear used by local fishermen is harming the ocean environment.
b. Big companies are using modern technology to catch large numbers of fish.

Rise of the Little Fish
a. It's important for the population of small fish to increase to ensure species diversity.
b. The rising number of small fish in the sea can harm the stability of our oceans.

A Future for Fish?
a. There are several things we can do to protect the ocean populations of big fish.
b. Governments need to take more responsibility for restoring the ocean's biodiversity.

B The flow chart below shows the effects of commercial fishing. Complete the missing information using the words and phrases in the box.

UNDERSTANDING A PROCESS

dropped	increased	too few	too many

Commercial fishing → The number of big fish has 1 _____. → There are 2 _____ predators left.

The number of small fish has 3 _____. ←

4 _____ small fish can damage the ocean's ecosystem. ←

C According to the writer, what are three possible solutions to overfishing? Note them in your own words.

IDENTIFYING PROBLEMS AND SOLUTIONS

1. _____

2. _____

3. _____

> **CRITICAL THINKING**   When you **evaluate an argument**, ask yourself: What information does the writer use to support their argument? For example, does the writer provide any facts or statistics? Is the information convincing?

D Work with a partner. Discuss the following questions about the reading passage.

CRITICAL THINKING: EVALUATING AN ARGUMENT

1. What statistics does the writer use to show that overfishing is a real problem?

2. How convincing is this argument? What other kinds of statistics or supporting information could the writer have provided?

DEVELOPING READING SKILLS

READING SKILL Interpreting Visual Information

Writers use charts, graphs, and maps to show information **visually**. This makes information easier to see.

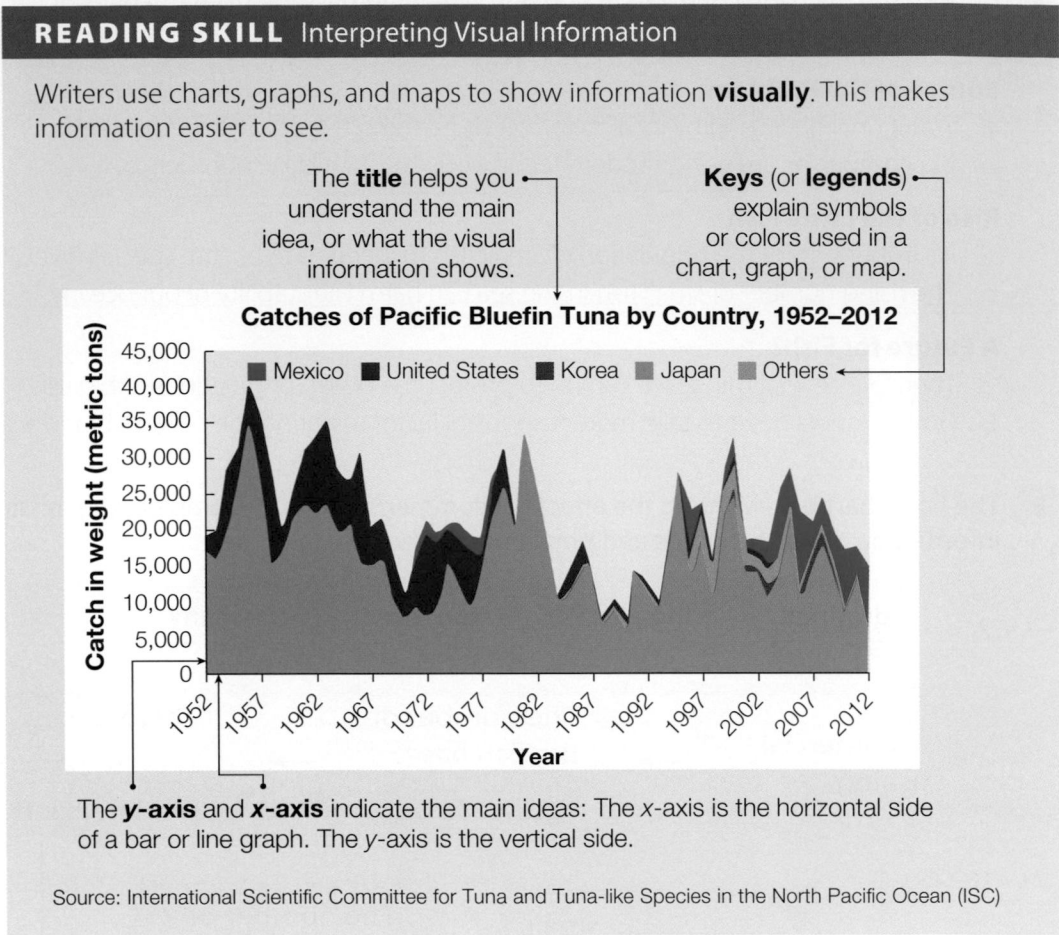

The **title** helps you understand the main idea, or what the visual information shows.

Keys (or **legends**) explain symbols or colors used in a chart, graph, or map.

Catches of Pacific Bluefin Tuna by Country, 1952–2012

Mexico ■ United States ■ Korea ■ Japan ■ Others

Catch in weight (metric tons)

Year

The **y-axis** and **x-axis** indicate the main ideas: The x-axis is the horizontal side of a bar or line graph. The y-axis is the vertical side.

Source: International Scientific Committee for Tuna and Tuna-like Species in the North Pacific Ocean (ISC)

INTERPRETING GRAPHS

A Look at the graph above and answer the following questions.

1. What does the graph show? What do the colors represent?

   _____

2. According to the graph, which countries were the only ones to fish for Pacific bluefin tuna before the 1970s?

   _____

3. Approximately how many metric tons of Pacific bluefin tuna were caught in 2012?

   _____

4. When was the lowest catch of Pacific bluefin tuna recorded? When was the highest?

   _____

INTERPRETING MAPS

B Look at the map on pages 70–71 again and answer the following questions.

1. Which areas are most affected by human activities? _____

2. Which areas are least affected by human activities? _____

Video

SAVING BLUEFIN TUNA

▲ A school of caged bluefin tuna

BEFORE VIEWING

LEARNING ABOUT
THE TOPIC

A Read the information about the bluefin tuna. Then answer the questions.

The bluefin tuna is one of the biggest and fastest fish in the world. There are three species: Atlantic, Pacific, and Southern. This blue- and silver-colored fish can grow to about 6.5 feet (2 meters) in length and 550 pounds (250 kilograms) in weight. It grows to this size by eating enormous quantities of smaller fish, crustaceans, squid, and eels. Its powerful fins help it swim up to 43 miles (70 kilometers) per hour. However, the bluefin is also known for its meat, which is often eaten raw, as sushi or sashimi. Due to the high demand for this fish, it's now an endangered species. In 2014, scientists reported that the Pacific bluefin tuna population was down to only 4 percent of what it was before commercial fishing began.

1. List two special characteristics of the bluefin tuna.

   _____

2. What is driving the high demand for the bluefin tuna?

   _____

3. What do you think can be done to help increase bluefin tuna populations?

   _____

B The words in **bold** below are used in the video. Match the correct form of each word to its definition.

> Fish **breed** by laying eggs or by giving birth to live fish.
>
> Some animals exist only in **captivity**, in places like zoos and wildlife parks.
>
> Most fish **hatchlings** are left on their own to survive immediately after leaving the egg.

1. _____ (n) a baby animal that has just come out from an egg

2. _____ (n) the state of being kept somewhere and not being free

3. _____ (v) to produce young animals

WHILE VIEWING

A ▶ Watch the video. How is Shukei Masuma helping the bluefin tuna population grow?

a. by breeding bluefins in tanks and pools until they can be returned to the sea

b. by removing adult bluefins from the wild and sending them to protected areas

c. by tracking bluefins in the wild to study their breeding behavior

B ▶ Watch the video again. Circle the correct words to complete the summary.

Shukei Masuma is trying to save the bluefin tuna from extinction by raising some in captivity. Bluefin tuna breed by [1] **laying eggs / giving birth to live fish**. Masuma faced difficulties in finding a stable water [2] **temperature / pressure** and the right [3] **tank size / food** for the baby fish. But after years of hard work, he succeeded. He shows ocean scientist Sylvia Earle the [4] **fins / eyes** of a fish as they begin to form.

AFTER VIEWING

A The narrator says that the Atlantic bluefin tuna population is now only one-fifth of its population in the 1970s. How does this compare with Pacific bluefin? Using the graph below, discuss these questions with a partner.

1. How does the Pacific bluefin population in 2012 compare with that in the early 1970s? Is this similar or different to the Atlantic bluefin?

2. How does the population in 2012 compare with that in the early 1960s?

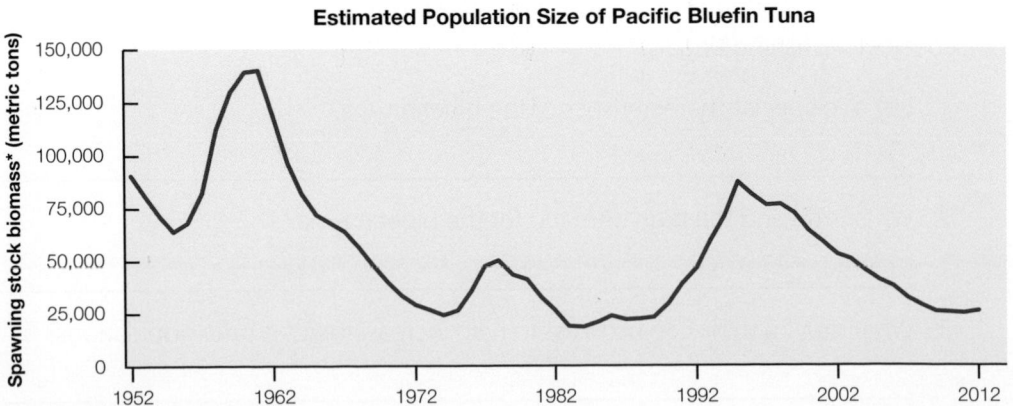

Estimated Population Size of Pacific Bluefin Tuna

*Population of adult fish capable of breeding

Source: ISC

Reading 2

PREPARING TO READ

A **A** The words and phrases in blue below are used in the reading passage on pages 80–81. Read their definitions and then complete each sentence with the correct form of the word or phrase.

> If something is **declining**, it is becoming less.
>
> If something is **definitely** true, it is for sure and without doubt.
>
> An **individual** is a single person.
>
> Something that is **essential** is extremely important or absolutely necessary.
>
> If you make an **informed** decision, you understand the facts of the situation.
>
> To **rely on** something means to need or depend on it.
>
> To make an **impact** on something means to have an effect or influence on it.
>
> If a problem is described as **severe**, it is very bad or serious.

1. If pollution is a global problem, what can we as _____ do about it?

2. Overfishing has led to _____ populations of predator fish. This is _____ having a negative effect on the ocean's ecosystem.

3. Protection of big fish species is _____ for the health of the oceans. If predator fish die out, the ocean's ecosystem will be unbalanced.

4. You can make _____ choices about seafood by researching which fish are endangered and which aren't.

5. Our love of sushi has led to _____ overfishing of bluefin tuna.

6. The use of modern equipment in commercial fishing has had a large _____ on the ocean's ecosystem.

7. Larger fish _____ smaller fish as a source of food.

B Discuss these questions with a partner.

1. What are three things you think are **essential** for the health of the planet?

2. How do you stay **informed** about environmental issues?

3. What are some negative **impacts** of global warming?

C Note some ideas about things you can do to help keep the oceans healthy. Share your ideas with a partner.

_____

_____

AN INTERVIEW WITH BARTON SEAVER

A Barton Seaver is a chef and conservationist[1] who wants our help to save the oceans. He believes that our eating choices have a direct **impact** on the ocean's health. In this interview, Seaver discusses how **individuals** can make a big difference by making **informed** choices.

Should people stop eating seafood?

B There are certain species that have been overfished and that people should **definitely** avoid for environmental reasons. But I don't think we need to stop eating seafood altogether. I believe that we can save the oceans while continuing to enjoy seafood. For example, some types of seafood, such as Alaskan salmon, come from well-managed fisheries. And others, such as farmed mussels and oysters, actually help to restore **declining** wild populations and clean up polluted waters.

What kind of seafood should people eat? What should they not eat?

C My general advice is to eat fish and shellfish that are lower on the food chain and that can be harvested[2] with little impact on the environment. Some examples include farmed mussels, clams and oysters, anchovies, sardines, and herring. People should not eat the bigger fish of the sea, like tuna, orange roughy, shark, sturgeon, and swordfish. Otherwise, we will face **severe** shortages of these species and upset the balance of life in the oceans.

Why did you choose to dedicate[3] your life to the ocean?

D I believe that the next great advance in human knowledge will come not from making new discoveries, but rather, from learning how we relate to our natural world. Humans are an **essential** part of nature, yet most humans do not have a very strong relationship with the world around them. I have dedicated myself to helping people understand our place on this planet through the foods that we eat.

Why do you believe people should care about the health of the oceans?

E The health of the oceans is directly linked to the health of people. The ocean provides most of the air that we breathe. It has a big effect on the weather that we **rely on** for crops and food production. It also provides a necessary and vital[4] diet for billions of people on the planet. So I don't usually say that I am trying to save the oceans. I prefer to say that I am trying to save the vital things that we rely on the ocean for.

Barton Seaver

| LEVEL 4 | **TOP PREDATORS** Animals that eat carnivores |

ATLANTIC BLUEFIN TUNA

ORANGE ROUGHY

ATLANTIC SALMON

[1]A **conservationist** is someone who works to protect the environment.
[2]When you **harvest** food, you gather it from the fields or the sea.
[3]When you **dedicate** yourself to something, you give it a lot of time and effort.
[4]Something that is **vital** is very important.

WHAT WE EAT MAKES A DIFFERENCE

When we eat predator fish, we increase our impact on the ocean. This is because predators sit at the top of the sea's food chain. They eat smaller fish and help to keep populations of other species from growing too large. At the bottom of the food chain are plants. They make their own food and produce all the oxygen in the ocean, just as plants on land do. Below is an illustration of an ocean food chain. The species can be classified into different levels.

F

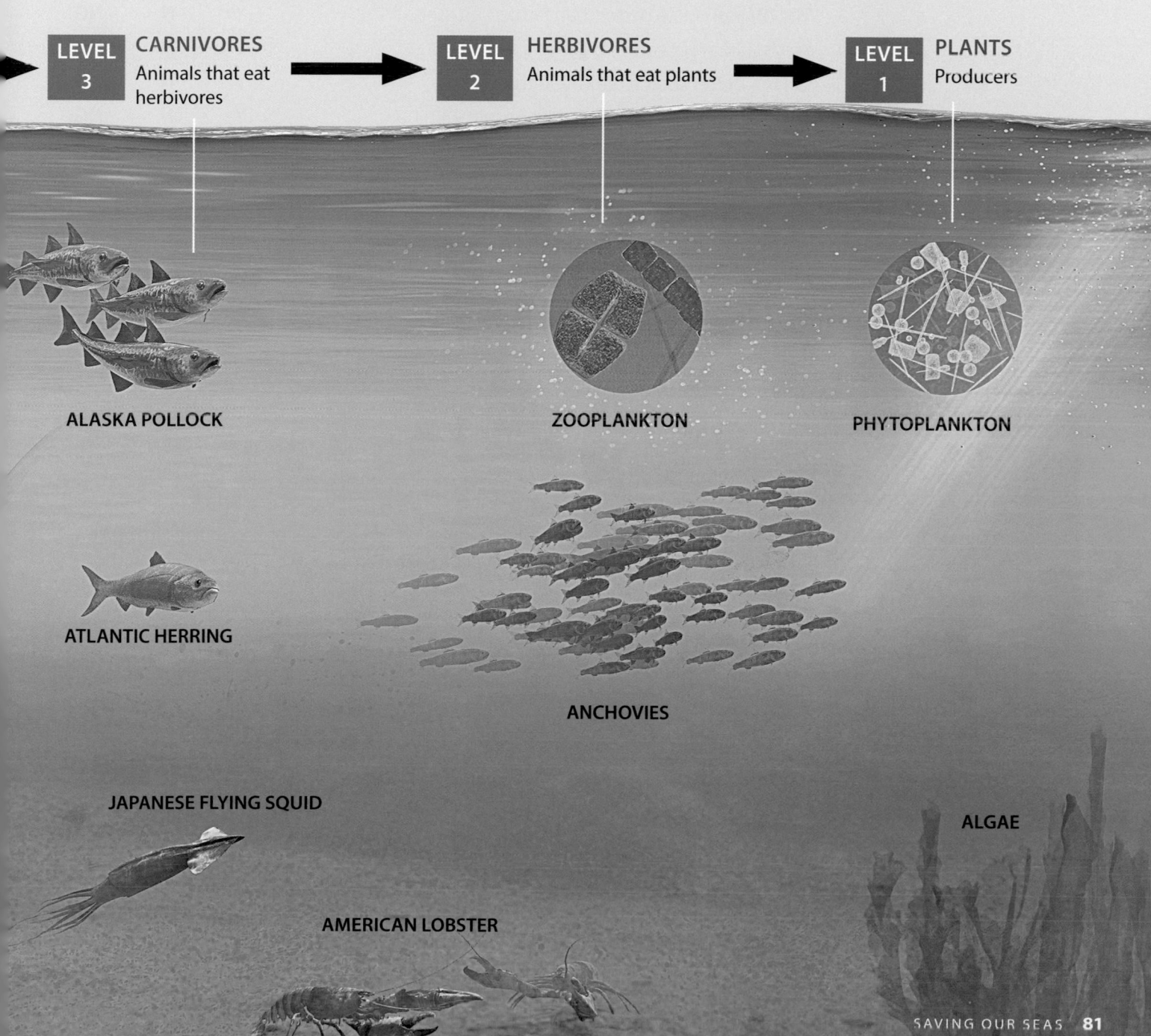

LEVEL 3 CARNIVORES
Animals that eat herbivores

LEVEL 2 HERBIVORES
Animals that eat plants

LEVEL 1 PLANTS
Producers

ALASKA POLLOCK

ZOOPLANKTON

PHYTOPLANKTON

ATLANTIC HERRING

ANCHOVIES

JAPANESE FLYING SQUID

ALGAE

AMERICAN LOBSTER

UNDERSTANDING THE READING

UNDERSTANDING
THE MAIN IDEA

A What is Barton Seaver's main message in his interview?

a. People should stop eating seafood so the ocean's ecosystem can be restored.

b. We need to protect the ocean because it provides most of the food that we eat.

c. Individuals can have a positive impact on the ocean by making good food choices.

IDENTIFYING
OPINIONS

B Based on his responses, would Barton Seaver agree with the following statements? Circle **Y** (Yes), **N** (No), or **NG** (Not Given) if there isn't enough information in the reading passage.

	Y	N	NG
1. It's OK to eat seafood from well-managed fisheries.	Y	N	NG
2. Fish farms are bad for the ocean.	Y	N	NG
3. Wild mussels taste better than farmed mussels.	Y	N	NG
4. We should avoid eating big fish.	Y	N	NG
5. Fish is a better source of protein than meat.	Y	N	NG
6. Most humans have a strong relationship with nature.	Y	N	NG
7. Healthy oceans will make people healthier.	Y	N	NG

INTERPRETING
VISUAL
INFORMATION

C Look at the illustration on pages 80–81 and answer the questions below.

1. What is one example of a top predator fish? _____

2. What kind of animals do top predators eat? _____

3. What is a herbivore? _____

4. What is one example of a herbivorous fish? _____

5. What is one species of fish that eats herbivores? _____

6. Why are plants called producers? _____

CRITICAL THINKING:
SYNTHESIZING

D Look at the information on pages 80–81 again. Which species of fish in the illustration would Barton Seaver say are OK and not OK to eat? List two examples of each in the chart below.

Fish that are OK to eat	Fish we should avoid
1.	1.
2.	2.

CRITICAL THINKING:
REFLECTING

E Based on what you have learned in this unit, do you plan to change any of your eating choices? Why or why not? Discuss with a partner.

UNIT REVIEW

Answer the following questions.

1. Which idea in this unit do you think is the most effective way to restore the ocean's biodiversity?

   _____

   _____

2. How and when could you use this unit's reading skill outside of class?

   _____

   _____

3. Do you remember the meanings of these words? Check (✓) the ones you know. Look back at the unit and review the ones you don't know.

   Reading 1:

   ☐ commercial   ☐ diverse **AWL**   ☐ doubled

   ☐ estimate **AWL**   ☐ quantity   ☐ reduce

   ☐ restore **AWL**   ☐ species   ☐ stable **AWL**

   ☐ survive **AWL**

   Reading 2:

   ☐ declining **AWL**   ☐ definitely **AWL**   ☐ essential

   ☐ impact **AWL**   ☐ individual **AWL**   ☐ informed

   ☐ rely on **AWL**   ☐ severe

VOCABULARY EXTENSION   UNIT 1

WORD FORMS   Adjectives and Nouns for Measurement

We use words like *deep, high, long*, and *wide* to talk about the size of an object. These words have an adjective and a noun form.

ADJECTIVE	NOUN
deep	*depth*
high	*height*
long	*length*
wide	*width*

A   Complete each sentence with a measurement word from the box above.

1. The _____ of a day on Earth is about 24 hours.

2. Some volcanoes are above ground, but some are _____ below the ocean surface.

3. The mountain Mauna Kea in the Pacific Ocean is over 10,000 meters _____. But only a third of it is visible above the ocean.

4. Growing to a _____ of over a hundred meters, the Californian redwoods are the tallest trees in the world.

5. The original Panama Canal was just over 30 meters _____, but many ships were too big to fit through it. To solve this problem, engineers increased the _____ of the Canal.

WORD PARTNERS   *run* + adverb/preposition

Some collocations are in the verb + adverb/preposition form. Below are definitions of common collocations with the verb *run*.

run into: to meet someone by chance

run out (of): to have no supplies left

run after: to follow or chase something or someone

run away (from): to leave somewhere because you are unhappy there

run up: to make something (e.g., a bill, debt, or score) become bigger

B   Match the sentence parts in the columns to complete each sentence.

_____ 1. I ran into   a. your problems, talk to someone about them.

_____ 2. I ran after   b. a huge bill at the hotel.

_____ 3. I ran up   c. my childhood friend this morning.

_____ 4. I ran out of   d. paint before I had finished the project.

_____ 5. Instead of running away from   e. the bus and got on it just in time.

VOCABULARY EXTENSION   UNIT 3

Some collocations are in adjective + noun form. Adding an adjective before the word *contribution* gives more information about the kind of contribution being described. Below are some common collocations with *contribution*.

positive contribution   small contribution

scientific contribution   large contribution

financial contribution   generous contribution

A Circle the correct word to complete each sentence.

1. Most crowdsourcing participants are not professional scientists. However, projects are carefully designed so that anyone can make a **generous** / **scientific** contribution.

2. By taking part in scientific online experiments, participants feel like they are making a **positive** / **financial** contribution to advancing human knowledge.

3. Crowdfunding projects raise money through **financial** / **positive** contributions from a large number of people.

4. Anyone who makes a contribution to a crowdfunding campaign, even if it is a **small** / **large** contribution, can make a difference.

5. People who make **scientific** / **large** contributions to crowdfunding campaigns receive certain rewards. For example, donors who gave over $2,299 to one campaign received a 3D printer.

WORD LINK *-al*

The suffix *-al* can mean "relating to." Add *-al* to some nouns to make them adjectives. For example, *global* means "relating to the whole world" (i.e., the globe).

B Complete each sentence using a word from the box below.

environmental	global	normal	tribal	virtual

1. Greenpeace and other _____ groups use the Internet to inform the public about pollution issues.

2. For many teenagers today, it is _____ to communicate with each other mainly through social media websites.

3. Some researchers think that _____ communities are not a good substitute for meeting people face-to-face.

4. English has become a(n) _____ language—there are English speakers in most countries around the world today.

5. Some _____ groups are concerned about the threat of logging to their traditional way of life.

VOCABULARY EXTENSION   UNIT 4

Some nouns can be made into adjectives by adding *-ial*, which means "connected or related to." For nouns ending in *-e* or *-y*, drop the *-e* or *-y* and add *-ial*.

NOUN	ADJECTIVE
commerce	*commercial*
industry	*industrial*

A   Complete each sentence using the adjective form of a word from the box below.

> commerce   face   finance   manager   office

1. The government's _____ definition of unemployment includes people who are "jobless, actively seeking work, and available to take a job."

2. According to one estimate, _____ fishing has wiped out 90 percent of large fish in the ocean.

3. A key _____ skill is the ability to motivate employees.

4. A(n) _____ advisor gives clients advice on how to manage their money.

5. _____ expressions are an important form of nonverbal communication.

WORD PARTNERS verb + *on*

Many collocations are formed with prepositions like *in, on,* or *out*. Below are definitions for common collocations with the preposition *on*.

rely on: to depend on someone or something

get on: to have a good relationship with someone

build on (success): to continue to achieve more success

take on (work): to begin to deal with more work

move on: to progress or become more modern

B   Complete each sentence using the correct form of a collocation from the box above.

1. We _____ the ocean for many things including food and oxygen.

2. In the past, local fishermen used traditional gear like spears and hooks to catch fish. Modern fishing technology has _____ a great deal since then.

3. Many well-known chefs _____ their success by publishing cookbooks and presenting cooking shows on TV.

4. Waiters who _____ well with customers often receive a bigger tip.

5. Since becoming the office manager, she has had to _____ new responsibilities.

GRAMMAR REFERENCE

UNIT 3
Language for Writing: Using the Present Perfect Tense

Subject	Have/Has (Not)	Verb (Past Participle)	Time Marker (optional)
I You We They	**have** **have not / haven't**	**been** here **slept** **called** him	since last year. for 24 hours. recently.
He She It	**has** **has not / hasn't**		

Time Markers

Use *since* + a point in time, *for* + a length of time, *in the* + time period to describe something that began in the past and continues to the present.

I've lived in Denmark **since** *2010.*
He hasn't been here **for** *three years.*
We've met a lot of people **in the past month**.

Use *already* in affirmative statements to emphasize that something happened at an unspecified time in the past.

I've watched that movie **already**. *She's* **already** *gone home.*

Use *recently* or *lately* to emphasize that something happened or didn't happen at an unspecified time in the recent past.

Sarah has called several times **recently**. *The team hasn't shown much improvement* **lately**.

Use the present perfect tense when the time in the past is not important.

I **have been** *to Fiji.*
He **has sung** *that song many times.*
Her work **has protected** *archaeological sites from looters.*

Past Participle Forms of Commonly Used Irregular Verbs

become—become	fall—fallen	read—read
begin—begun	find—found	say—said
bring—brought	get—gotten	see—seen
build—built	give—given	speak—spoken
buy—bought	have—had	take—taken
choose—chosen	hear—heard	tell—told
do—done	know—known	think—thought
eat—eaten	make—made	write—written

EDITING CHECKLIST

Use the checklist to find errors in your writing task for each unit.

	WRITING TASK	
	1	2
1. Is the first word of every sentence capitalized?		
2. Does every sentence end with the correct punctuation?		
3. Do your subjects and verbs agree?		
4. Are commas used in the right places?		
5. Do all possessive nouns have an apostrophe?		
6. Are all proper nouns capitalized?		
7. Is the spelling of places, people, and other proper nouns correct?		
8. Did you check for frequently confused words?		

Brief Writer's Handbook

Understanding the Writing Process: The Seven Steps

The Assignment

Imagine that you have been given the following assignment: *Write a definition paragraph about an everyday item.*

What should you do first? What should you do second, third, and so on? There are many ways to write, but most good writers follow certain general steps in the writing process.

Look at this list of steps. Which ones do you usually do? Which ones have you never done?

STEP 1: Choose a topic.

STEP 2: Brainstorm.

STEP 3: Outline.

STEP 4: Write the first draft.

STEP 5: Get feedback from a peer.

STEP 6: Revise the first draft.

STEP 7: Proofread the final draft.

Now you will see how one student went through all the steps to do the assignment. First, read the final paragraph that Susan gave her teacher. Read the teacher's comments as well.

Example Paragraph 1

Gumbo

The dictionary definition of *gumbo* does not make gumbo sound as delicious as it really is. The dictionary defines gumbo as a "thick soup made in south Louisiana." However, anyone who has tasted this delicious dish knows that this definition is too bland to describe gumbo. It is true that gumbo is a thick soup, but it is much more than that. Gumbo, one of the most popular of all Cajun dishes, is made with different kinds of seafood or meat mixed with vegetables, such as green peppers and onions. For example, seafood gumbo contains shrimp and crab. Other kinds of gumbo include chicken, sausage, or turkey. Regardless of the ingredients in gumbo, this regional delicacy is very delicious.

Teacher comments:

100/A+   Excellent paragraph!
I enjoyed reading about gumbo. Your paragraph is very well written. All the sentences relate to one single topic. I really like the fact that you used so many connectors—however, such as.

Now look at the steps that Susan went through to compose the paragraph that you just read.

Steps in the Writing Process
Step 1: Choose a Topic
Susan chose gumbo as her topic. This is what she wrote about her choice.

○ When I first saw the assignment, I did not know what to write about. I did not think I was going to be able to find a good topic.

First, I tried to think of something that I could define. It could not be something that was really simple like television or a car. Everyone already knows what they are. I thought that I should choose something that most people might not know.

I tried to think of general areas like sports, machines, and inventions. However, I chose food as my general area. Everyone likes food.

○ Then I had to find one kind of food that not everyone knows. For me, that was not too difficult. My family is from Louisiana, and the food in Louisiana is special. It is not the usual food that most Americans eat. One of the dishes we eat a lot in Louisiana is gumbo, which is a kind of thick soup. I thought gumbo would be a good topic for a definition paragraph because not many people know it, and it is sort of easy for me to write a definition for this food.

Another reason that gumbo is a good choice for a definition paragraph is that I know a lot about this kind of food. I know how to make it, I know what the ingredients are, and I know what it tastes like. It is much easier to write about something that I know than about something that I do not know about.

○ After I was sure that gumbo was going to be my topic, I went on to the next step, which is brainstorming.

Susan's notes about choosing her topic

Step 2: Brainstorm

The next step for Susan was to brainstorm ideas about her topic.

In this step, you write down every idea that pops into your head about your topic. Some of these ideas will be good, and some will be bad—write them all down. The main purpose of brainstorming is to write down as many ideas as you can think of. If one idea looks especially good, you might circle that idea or put a check mark next to it. If you write down an idea and you know right away that you are not going to use it, you can cross it out.

Look at Susan's brainstorming diagram on the topic of gumbo.

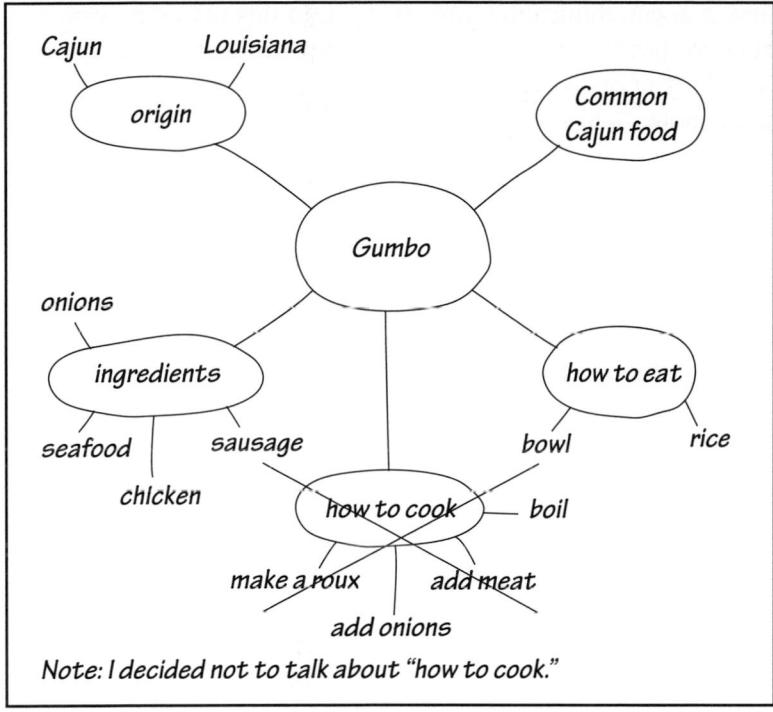

Susan's brainstorming diagram

Step 3: Outline

At this point, some writers want to start writing, but that is not the best plan. After you brainstorm your ideas, the next step is to make an outline. An outline helps you organize how you will present your information. It helps you see which areas of the paragraph are strong and which are weak.

After brainstorming, Susan studied her list of ideas. She then made a simple outline of what her paragraph might look like. Some writers prepare very detailed outlines, but many writers just make a list of the main points and some of the details for each main point.

Read the outline that Susan wrote.

What is gumbo?
1. A simple definition of gumbo.
2. A longer definition of gumbo.
3. A list of the different ingredients of gumbo.
    A. seafood or meat
    B. with vegetables (onions)
    C. seafood gumbo
4. How gumbo is served.

Susan's outline

As you can see, this outline is very basic. There are also some problems. For example, Susan repeats some items in different parts of the outline. In addition, she does not have a concluding sentence. These errors will probably be corrected at the first draft step, the peer editing step, or the final draft step.

Step 4: Write the First Draft

Next, Susan wrote a first draft. In this step, you use the information from your outline and from your brainstorming session to write a first draft. This first draft may contain many errors, such as misspellings, incomplete ideas, and incorrect punctuation. At this point, do not worry about correcting the errors. The main goal is to put your ideas into sentences.

You may feel that you do not know what you think about the topic yet. In this case, it may be difficult for you to write, but it is important to start the process of writing. Sometimes writing helps you think, and as soon as you form a new thought, you can write it down.

Read Susan's first draft, including her notes to herself.

Introduction is weak ??? Use dictionary!

(Rough draft)
Susan Mims

Do you know what gumbo is. It's a seafood soup. However, gumbo is really more than a kind of soup, it's special. ???

Gumbo is one of the most popular of all Cajun dishes. es

Combine { *It's made with various kinds of seafood or meet. meat*
This is mixed with vegetables such as onions. green peppers

Combine { *Seafood Gumbo is made with shrimp and crab.*
Also chicken, sausage, and turkey, etc. Regardless ok??? of what is in Gumbo, it's usually served in a bowl over the rice.
— Is this correct? Ask teacher!

Susan's first draft

What do you notice about this first draft? Here are a few things that a good writer should pay attention to:

- First of all, remember that this paper is not the final draft. Even native speakers who are good writers usually write more than one draft. You will have a chance to revise the paper and make it better.

- Look at the circles, question marks, and writing in the margin. These are notes that Susan made to herself about what to change, add, or reconsider.

- Remember that the paper will go through the peer-editing process later. Another reader will help you make your meaning clear and will look for errors.

In addition to the language errors that writers often make in the first draft, the handwriting is usually not neat. Sometimes it is so messy that only the writer can read it!

Step 5: Get Feedback from a Peer

Peer editing a draft is a critical step toward the final goal of excellent writing. Sometimes it is difficult for writers to see the weaknesses in their own writing, so receiving advice from another writer can be very helpful.

Ask a colleague, friend, or classmate to read your writing and to offer suggestions about how to improve it. Some people do not like criticism, but constructive criticism is always helpful for writers. Remember that even professional writers have editors, so do not be embarrassed to receive help.

Susan exchanged papers with another student, Jim, in her class. On the next page is the peer editing sheet that Jim completed about Susan's paragraph. Read the questions and answers.

Peer Editing Sheet

Writer: __Susan__   Date: __2-14__

Peer Editor: __Jim__

1. What is the general topic of the paper? __gumbo__

2. What is the writer's purpose? (in 15 words or less)

   __to define gumbo__

3. Is the paragraph indented? ☑ yes   ☐ no

4. How many sentences are there? __6__

5. Is the first word of every sentence capitalized? ☑ yes   ☐ no
   If you answered *no*, circle the problem(s) on the paper.

6. Does every sentence end with correct punctuation? ☐ yes   ☑ no
   If you answered *no*, circle the problem(s) on the paper.

7. Are there any other capitalization or punctuation errors? ☑ yes   ☐ no
   If you answered *yes*, circle the problem(s) on the paper.

8. Write the topic sentence here.

   __You have two sentences: Do you know what gumbo is. It is a seafood soup.__

9. Do you think the topic sentence is good for this paragraph? Comments?

   __No, you need one sentence that introduces your topic and purpose better.__

10. Does the paragraph talk about just one topic? ☑ yes   ☐ no

    If you answered *no*, what is the extra topic? _____

    In what sentence is this extra topic introduced? _____

11. Does every sentence have a verb? ☐ yes ☑ no

   If you answered *no*, circle the error(s) on the paper.

12. Write any mistakes that you found. Add appropriate corrections.

   Error 1: _it's-don't use contractions in formal writing_

   Correction: _it is_

   Error 2: _etc.-don't use this_

   Correction: _You should list all the kinds._

   Error 3: _____

   Correction: _____

13. Did you have any trouble understanding this paragraph? ☐ yes ☑ no

   If you answered *yes*, tell where and/or why.

   _____

14. What questions do you have about the content? What other information should be in this paragraph?

   How do you make gumbo? Is it easy to cook? Why do you think people started making gumbo?

15. What is your opinion of the writing of this paragraph?

   It is good, but the concluding sentence gives new information. It does not conclude! Also,

   do not repeat the word "gumbo" so much. Do not use "is" so much! Use other verbs.

16. What is your opinion of the content of this paragraph?

   I like the topic. I think I ate gumbo at a restaurant once.

Step 6: Revise the First Draft

In this step, you will see how Susan used the suggestions and information to revise her paragraph. This step consists of three parts:

1. React to the comments on the peer editing sheet.

2. Reread the paragraph and make changes.

3. Rewrite the paragraph one more time.

Here is what Susan wrote about the changes she decided to make.

> I read my paragraph again several times. Each time I read it, I found things that I wanted to change in some way. Sometimes I corrected an obvious error. Other times I added words to make my writing clear to the reader. Based on Jim's suggestion, I used "this delicious dish" and other expressions instead of repeating "gumbo" so many times.
>
> I used some of Jim's suggestions, but I did not use all of them. I thought that some of his questions were interesting, but the answers were not really part of the purpose of this paragraph, which was to define gumbo.
>
> I was happy that the peer editor was able to understand all my ideas fully. To me, this means that my writing is good enough.

Susan's notes about changes she decided to make

Step 7: Proofread the Final Draft

Most of the hard work should be over by now. In this step, the writer pretends to be a brand-new reader who has never seen the paper before. The writer reads the paper to see if the sentences and ideas flow smoothly.

Read Susan's final paper again on page 89. Notice any changes in vocabulary, grammar, spelling, or punctuation that she made at this stage.

Of course, the very last step is to turn the paper in to your teacher and hope that you get a good grade!

Editing Your Writing

While you must be comfortable writing quickly, you also need to be comfortable with improving your work. Writing an assignment is never a one-step process. For even the most gifted writers, it is often a multiple-step process. When you were completing your assignments in this book, you probably made some changes to your work to make it better. However, you may not have fixed all of the errors. The paper that you turned in to your teacher is called a **first draft,** which is sometimes referred to as a **rough draft.**

A first draft can almost always be improved. One way to improve your writing is to ask a classmate, friend, or teacher to read it and make suggestions. Your reader may discover that one of your paragraphs is missing a topic sentence, that you have made grammar mistakes, or that your essay needs different vocabulary choices. You may not always like or agree with the comments from a reader, but being open to changes will make you a better writer.

This section will help you become more familiar with how to identify and correct errors in your writing.

Step 1

Below is a student's first draft for a timed writing. The writing prompt for this assignment, was "Many schools now offer classes online. Which do you prefer and why?" As you read the first draft, look for areas that need improvement and write your comments. For example, does every sentence have a subject and a verb? Does the writer always use the correct verb tense and punctuation? Does the paragraph have a topic sentence with controlling ideas? Is the vocabulary suitable for the intended audience? What do you think of the content?

The Online Courses

Online courses are very popular at my university. I prefered traditional face-to-face classes. At my university, students have a choice between courses that are taught online in a virtual classroom and the regular kind of classroom. I know that many students prefer online classes, but I cannot adjust to that style of educate. For me, is important to have a professor who explains the material to everyone "live" and then answer any questions that we have. Sometimes students might think they understand the material until the professor questions, and then we realize that we did not understand everything. At that moment, the professor then offers other explanation to help bridge the gap. I do not see this kind of spontaneous learning and teaching can take place online. I have never taken an online course until now. Some of my friends like online courses because they can take the class at his own convenience instead of have to assist class at a set time. However, these supposed conveniences are not outweigh the educational advantages that traditional face-to-face classes offer.

Step 2

Read the teacher comments on the first draft of "The Online Courses." Are these the same things that you noticed?

Your title is OK. Any other ideas?

The Online Courses

Combine first two sentences.

Online courses are very popular at my university. I prefered traditional face-to-face

classes. At my university, students have a choice between courses that are taught online in a virtual

Give more details about CLASS3ROOM. Describe it.

classroom and the regular kind of classroom. I know that many students prefer online classes,

WORD FORM SUBJ?

but I cannot adjust to that style of educate. For me, is important to have a professor who explains

the material to everyone "live" and then answer any questions that we have. Sometimes students

POSES A QUESTION

might think they understand the material until the professor questions, and then we realize that

we did not understand everything. At that moment, the professor then offers other explanation

Which gap???   HOW?

to help bridge the gap. I do not see this kind of spontaneous learning and teaching can take place

Purpose of this sentence? Connected to the topic?

online. I have never taken an online course until now. Some of my friends like online courses

because they can take the class at his own convenience instead of have to assist class at a set

Add more reasons here!

time. However, these supposed conveniences are not outweigh the educational advantages that

traditional face-to-face classes offer.

You have some very good ideas in this paragraph. Your topic sentence and concluding sentence are good. Your title is OK, but can you spice it up? It's rather plain right now. Check to make sure that all of your sentences are relevant. Also, I've circled several grammar errors. You need to change these. I also recommend adding some info in a few places. All in all, it's a good paragraph. I understand why you don't like online courses. The more specific reasons you can provide, the better you can convince your readers.

Step 3

Now read the writer's second draft of the paragraph. How is it the same as the first draft? How is it different? Did the writer fix all the sentence mistakes?

Online Courses

Online courses are very popular at my university but I prefer traditional face-to-face classes. At my university students have a choice between courses that are taught online in a virtual classroom and the regular kind of classroom with a room, a professor, and students in chairs. I know that many students prefer online classes, but I cannot adjust to that style of education. For me, it is important to have a professor who explains the material to everyone "live" and then answers any questions that we might have. Sometimes students might think they understand the material until the professor poses a question, and then we realize that we did not understand everything. At that moment, the professor then offers another explanation to help bridge the gap between our knowledge and the truth. I do not see how this kind of spontaneous leaerning and teaching can take place online. Some of my friends like online courses because they can take the class at their own convenience instead of having to attend class at a set time. They also like to save transportation money and time. However, these supposed conveniences do not outweigh the many educational advantages that traditional face-to-face classes offer.

Capitalization Activities
Basic Capitalization Rules

1. Always capitalize the first word of a sentence.

   Today is not Sunday.

   It is not Saturday either.

   Do you know today's date?

2. Always capitalize the word *I* no matter where it is in a sentence.

   John brought the dessert, and **I** brought some drinks.

   I want some tea.

   The winners of the contest were Ned and **I**.

3. Capitalize proper nouns—the names of specific people, places, or things. Capitalize a person's title, including Mr., Mrs., Ms., and Dr. Compare these example pairs.

   Proper nouns: When our teacher **M**r. **H**ill visited his home state of **A**rizona, he took a short trip to see the **G**rand **C**anyon.

   Common nouns: When our teacher visited his home state, he saw many mountains and canyons.

   Proper nouns: The **S**tatue of **L**iberty is located on **L**iberty **I**sland in **N**ew **Y**ork.

   Common nouns: There is a famous statue on that island, isn't there?

4. Capitalize names of countries and other geographic areas. Capitalize the names of people from those areas. Capitalize the names of languages.

   People from **B**razil are called **B**razilians. They speak **P**ortuguese.

   People from **G**ermany are called **G**ermans. They speak **G**erman.

5. Capitalize titles of works, such as books, movies, and pieces of art. If you look at the example paragraphs in this book, you will notice that each of them begins with a title. In a title, pay attention to which words begin with a capital letter and which words do not.

Gumbo	*A Lesson in Friendship*	*An Immigrant in the Family*
The King and I	*The Tale of Pinocchio*	*Love at First Sight*

   The rules for capitalizing titles are easy.

   - Always capitalize the first letter of a title.

   - If the title has more than one word, capitalize all the words that have meaning (content words).

   - Do not capitalize small (function) words, such as *a, an, and, the, in, with, on, for, to, above,* and *or.*

Capitalization Activities

ACTIVITY 1

Circle the words that have capitalization errors. Make the corrections above the errors.

1. the last day to sign up for the trip to sao paolo is this Thursday.

2. does jill live in west bay apartments, too?

3. the flight to Vancouver left late Saturday night and arrived early Sunday morning.

4. My sister has two daughters. Their names are rachel and rosalyn.

5. one of the most important sporting events is the world cup.

ACTIVITY 2

Complete these statements. Be sure to use correct capitalization.

1. *U.S.A.* stands for the United _____ of _____ .

2. The seventh month of the year is _____ .

3. _____ is the capital of Brazil.

4. One of the most popular brands of jeans is _____ .

5. The first person to walk on the moon was named _____ .

6. Parts of Europe were destroyed in _____ (1914–18).

7. My favorite restaurant is _____ .

8. Beijing is the largest city in _____ .

9. The winter months are _____ , _____ , and _____ .

10. The last movie that I saw was _____ .

ACTIVITY 3

Read the following titles. Rewrite them with correct capitalization.

1. my favorite food _____

2. living in montreal _____

3. the best restaurant in town _____

4. my best friend's new car _____

5. a new trend in Hollywood _____

6. why i left my country _____

7. my side of the mountain _____

8. no more room for a friend _____

Read the following paragraph. Circle the capitalization errors and make corrections above the errors.

A visit to Cuba

according to an article in last week's issue of *time*, the prime minister of canada will visit cuba soon in order to establish better economic ties between the two countries. because the united states does not have a history of good relations with cuba, canada's recent decision may result in problems between washington and ottawa. In an interview, the canadian prime minister indicated that his country was ready to reestablish some sort of cooperation with cuba and that canada would do so as quickly as possible. there is no doubt that this new development will be discussed at the opening session of congress next tuesday.

Read the following paragraph. Circle the capitalization errors and make corrections above the errors.

crossing the atlantic from atlanta

it used to be difficult to travel directly from atlanta to europe, but this is certainly not the case nowadays. union airways offers several daily flights to london. jetwings express offers flights every day to frankfurt and twice a week to berlin. other european air carriers that offer direct flights from atlanta to europe are valuair and luxliner. However, the airline with the largest number of direct flights to any european city is not a european airline. smead airlines, which is a new and rising airline in the united states, offers 17 flights a day to 12 european cities, including paris, london, frankfurt, zurich, rome, and athens.

Read the following paragraph. Circle the capitalization errors and make corrections above the errors.

Example Paragraph 4

my beginnings in foreign languages

I have always loved foreign languages. When I was in tenth grade, I took my first foreign language class. It was french I. My teacher was named mrs. montluzin. She was a wonderful teacher who inspired me to develop my interest in foreign languages. Before I finished high school, I took a second year of french and one year of spanish. I wish my high school had offered latin or greek, but the small size of the school body prevented this. Over the years since I graduated from high school, I have lived and worked abroad. I studied arabic when I lived in saudi arabia, japanese in japan, and malay in malaysia. Two years ago, I took a german class in the united states. Because of recent travels to uzbekistan and kyrgyzstan, which are two republics from the former soviet union, I have a strong desire to study russian. I hope that my love of learning foreign languages will continue.

Punctuation Activities
End Punctuation

The three most common punctuation marks found at the end of English sentences are the **period**, the **question mark**, and the **exclamation point**. It is important to know how to use all three of them correctly. Of these three, however, the period is by far the most commonly used punctuation mark.

1. **period** (.) A period is used at the end of a declarative sentence.

   This sentence is a declarative sentence.

   This sentence is not a question.

   All three of these sentences end with a period.

2. **question mark** (?) A question mark is used at the end of a question.

   Is this idea difficult?

   Is it hard to remember the name of this mark?

   How many questions are in this group?

3. **exclamation point** (!) An exclamation point is used at the end of an exclamation. It is less common than the other two marks.

> I cannot believe you think this topic is difficult**!**
>
> This is the best writing book in the world**!**
>
> Now I understand all of these examples**!**

ACTIVITY 1

Add the correct end punctuation.

1. Congratulations

2. Do most people think that the governor was unaware of the theft

3. Do not open your test booklet until you are told to do so

4. Will the president attend the meeting

5. Jason put the dishes in the dishwasher and then watched TV

ACTIVITY 2

Look at an article in any English newspaper or magazine. Circle every end punctuation mark. Then answer these questions.

1. How many final periods are there? _____ (or _____ %)

2. How many final question marks are there? _____ (or _____ %)

3. How many final exclamation points are there? _____ (or _____ %)

4. What is the total number of sentences? _____

Use this last number to calculate the percentages for each of the categories. Does the period occur most often?

Commas

The comma has several different functions in English. Here are some of the most common ones.

1. A comma separates a list of three or more things. There should be a comma between the items in a list.

> He speaks French and English. (No comma is needed because there are only two items.)
>
> She speaks French, English, and Chinese.

2. A comma separates two sentences when there is a combining word (coordinating conjunction) such as *and, but, or, so, for, nor,* and *yet.* The easy way to remember these conjunctions is *FANBOYS (for, and, nor, but, or, yet, so).*

> Six people took the course, but only five of them passed the test.
>
> Sammy bought the cake, and Paul paid for the ice cream.
>
> Students can register for classes in person, or they may submit their applications by mail.

3. A comma is used to separate an introductory word or phrase from the rest of the sentence.

> In conclusion, doctors are advising people to take more vitamins.
>
> First, you will need a pencil.
>
> Because of the heavy rains, many of the roads were flooded.
>
> Finally, add the nuts to the batter.

4. A comma is used to separate an appositive from the rest of the sentence. An appositive is a word or group of words that renames a noun before it. An appositive provides additional information about the noun.

subject (noun) | appositive | verb

Washington, the first president of the United States, was a clever military leader.

In this sentence, the phrase *the first president of the United States* is an appositive. This phrase renames or explains the noun *Washington*.

5. A comma is sometimes used with adjective clauses. An adjective clause usually begins with a relative pronoun *(who, that, which, whom, whose, whoever,* or *whomever)*. We use a comma when the information in the clause is unnecessary or extra. (This is also called a nonrestrictive clause.)

The book <u>that is on the teacher's desk</u> is the main book for this class.

(Here, when you say "the book," the reader does not know which book you are talking about, so the information in the adjective clause is necessary. In this case, do not set off the adjective clause with a comma.)

The History of Korea, <u>which is on the teacher's desk,</u> is the main book for this class.

(The name of the book is given, so the information in the adjective clause is not necessary to help the reader identify the book. In this case, you must use commas to show that the information in the adjective clause is extra, or nonrestrictive.)

ACTIVITY 3

Add commas as needed in these sentences. Some sentences may be correct, and others may need more than one comma.

1. For the past fifteen years Mary Parker has been both the director and producer of all the plays at this theater.

2. Despite all the problems we had on our vacation we managed to have a good time.

3. I believe the best countries to visit in Africa are Senegal Tunisia and Ghana.

4. She believes the best countries to visit in Africa are Senegal and Tunisia.

5. The third step in this process is to grate the carrots and the potatoes.

6. Third grate the carrots and the potatoes.

7. Blue green and red are strong colors. For this reason they are not appropriate for a living room wall.

8. Without anyone to teach foreign language classes next year the school will be unable to offer French Spanish or German.

9. The NEQ 7000 the very latest computer from Electron Technologies is not selling very well.

10. Because of injuries neither Carl nor Jamil two of the best players on the football team will be able to play in tomorrow's game.

11. The job interview is for a position at Mills Trust Company which is the largest company in this area.

12. The job interview is for a position at a large company that has more than 1,000 employees in this area.

13. Kevin's birthday is January 18 which is the same day that Laura and Greg have their birthdays.

14. Martina Navratilova whom most tennis fans refer to only as Martina dominated women's tennis for years.

15. My brother who lives in San Salvador has two children. (I have several brothers.)

16. My brother who lives in San Salvador has two children. (I have only one brother.)

17. This flight is leaving for La Paz which is the first of three stops that the plane will make.

18. No one knows the name of the person who will take over the committee in January so there have been many rumors about this.

19. Greenfield Central Bank the most recent bank to open a branch here in our area has tried to establish a branch here for years.

20. On the right side of the living room an antique radio sits on top of a glass table that also has a flowerpot a photo of a baby and a magazine.

Apostrophes

Apostrophes have two basic uses in English. They indicate either a contraction or possession.

Contractions: Use an apostrophe in a contraction in place of the letter or letters that have been deleted.

> He's (he is *or* he has), they're (they are), I've (I have), we'd (we would *or* we had)

Possession: Use an apostrophe to indicate possession. Add an apostrophe and the letter *s* after the word. If a plural word already ends in *s*, then just add an apostrophe.

> Gandhi's role in the history of India
> Yesterday's paper
> the boy's books (One boy has some books.)
> the boys' books (Several boys have one or more books.)

ACTIVITY 4

Correct the apostrophe errors in these sentences.

1. I am going to Victors birthday party on Saturday.

2. My three cousins house is right next to Mr. Wilsons house.

3. Hardly anyone remembers Stalins drastic actions in the early part of the last century.

4. It goes without saying that wed be better off without so much poverty in this world.

5. The reasons that were given for the childrens bad behavior were unbelievable.

Quotation Marks

Below are three of the most common uses for quotation marks.

1. To mark the exact words that were spoken by someone:

    The king said, "I refuse to give up my throne." (The period is inside the quotation marks.)*

    "None of the solutions is correct," said the professor. (The comma is inside the quotation marks.)*

    The king said that he refuses to give up his throne. (No quotation marks are needed because the sentence does not include the king's exact words. This style is called indirect speech.)

    * Note that the comma separates the verb that tells the form of communications (*said, announced, wrote*) and the quotation.

2. To mark language that a writer has borrowed from another source:

    The dictionary defines gossip as an "informal conversation, often about other people's private affairs," but I would add that it is usually malicious.

    This research concludes that there was "no real reason to expect this computer software program to produce good results with high school students."

    According to an article in *The San Jose Times,* about half of the money was stolen. (No quotes are necessary here because it is a summary of information rather than exact words from the article.)

3. To indicate when a word or phrase is being used in a special way:

    The king believed himself to be the leader of a democracy, so he allowed the prisoner to choose his method of dying. According to the king, allowing this kind of "democracy" showed that he was indeed a good ruler.

ACTIVITY 5

Add quotation marks where necessary. Remember the rules for placing commas, periods, and question marks inside or outside the quotation marks.

1. As I was leaving the room, I heard the teacher say, Be sure to study Chapter 7.

2. It is impossible to say that using dictionaries is useless. However, according to research published in the latest issue of the *General Language Journal,* dictionary use is down. I found the article's statement that 18.3 percent of students do not own a dictionary and 37.2 percent never use their dictionary (p. 75) to be rather shocking.

    Source: Wendt, John "Dictionary Use by Language Students," *General Language Journal* 3 (2007): 72-101.

3. My fiancée says that if I buy her a huge diamond ring, this would be a sign that I love her. I would like to know if there is a less expensive sign that would be a sure sign of my love for her.

4. When my English friend speaks of a heat wave just because the temperature reaches over 80°, I have to laugh because I come from Thailand, where we have sunshine most of the year. The days when we have to dress warmly are certainly few, and some people wear shorts outside almost every month of the year.

5. The directions on the package read, Open carefully. Add contents to one glass of warm water. Drink just before bedtime.

Semicolons

The semicolon is used most often to combine two related sentences. Once you get used to using the semicolon, you will find that it is a very easy and useful punctuation tool to vary the sentences in your writing.

- Use a semicolon when you want to connect two simple sentences.

- The function of a semicolon is similar to that of a period. However, in order to use a semicolon, there must be a relationship between the sentences.

> Joey loves to play tennis. He has been playing since he was ten years old.

> Joey loves to play tennis; he has been playing since he was ten years old.

Both sentence pairs are correct. The main difference is that the semicolon in the second example signals the relationship between the ideas in the two sentences. Notice also that *he* is not capitalized in the second example.

ACTIVITY 6

The following sentences use periods for separation. Rewrite the sentences. Replace the periods with semicolons and make any other necessary changes.

1. Gretchen and Bob have been friends since elementary school. They are also next-door neighbors.

   _____

2. The test was complicated. No one passed it.

   _____

3. Tomatoes are necessary for a garden salad. Peas are not.

   _____

4. Mexico lies to the south of the United States. Canada lies to the north.

   _____

Look at a copy of an English newspaper or magazine. Circle all the semicolons on a page. The number should be relatively small.

NOTE: If the topic of the article is technical or complex, there is a greater chance of finding semicolons. Semicolons are not usually used in informal or friendly writing. Thus, you might see a semicolon in an article about heart surgery or educational research, but not in an ad for a household product or an e-mail or text message to a friend.

Editing for Errors

ACTIVITY 8

Find the 14 punctuation errors in this paragraph and make corrections above the errors.

Example Paragraph 5

An Unexpected Storm

Severe weather is a constant possibility all over the globe; but we never really expect our own area to be affected However last night was different At about ten o'clock a tornado hit Lucedale This violent weather destroyed nine homes near the downtown area In addition to these nine houses that were completely destroyed many others in the area had heavy damage Amazingly no one was injured in last nights terrible storm Because of the rapid reaction of state and local weather watchers most of the areas residents saw the warnings that were broadcast on television

ACTIVITY 9

Find the 15 punctuation errors in this paragraph and make corrections above the errors.

Example Paragraph 6

Deserts

Deserts are some of the most interesting places on earth A desert is not just a dry area it is an area that receives less than ten inches of rainfall a year About one-fifth of the earth is composed of deserts Although many people believe that deserts are nothing but hills of sand this is not true In reality deserts have large rocks mountains canyons and even lakes For instance only about ten percent of the Sahara Desert the largest desert on the earth is sand

Find the 15 punctuation errors in this paragraph and make corrections above the errors.

Example Paragraph 7

A Review

I Wish I Could Have Seen His Face Marilyn Kings latest novel is perhaps her greatest triumph In this book King tells the story of the Lamberts a poor family that struggles to survive despite numerous hardships. The Lambert family consists of five strong personalities. Michael Lambert has trouble keeping a job and Naomi earns very little as a maid at a hotel The three children range in age from nine to sixteen. Dan Melinda and Zeke are still in school This well-written novel allows us to step into the conflict that each of the children has to deal with. Only a writer as talented as King could develop five independent characters in such an outstanding manner The plot has many unexpected turns and the outcome of this story will not disappoint readers While King has written several novels that won international praise *I Wish I Could IIave Seen IIis Face* is in many ways better than any of her previous works.

Additional Grammar Activities
Verb Tense

ACTIVITY 1

Fill in the blanks with the verb that best completes the sentence. Be sure to use the correct form of the verb. Use the following verbs: *like, cut, break, stir,* and *spread.*

Example Paragraph 8

A Simple Sandwich

Making a tuna salad sandwich is not difficult. Put two cans of flaked tuna in a medium-sized bowl. With a fork, _____ the fish apart. _____ up a large white onion or two small yellow onions. _____ in one-third cup of mayonnaise. Then add salt and pepper to taste. Some people _____ to mix

pieces of boiled eggs into their salad. Once you finish making the salad,

_____ it between two slices of bread. Now you are ready to

eat your easy-to-make treat.

ACTIVITY 2

Fill in the blanks with the correct form of any appropriate verb.

Example Paragraph 9

Who Killed Kennedy?

One of the most infamous moments in U.S. history _____

in 1963. In that year, President John F. Kennedy _____

assassinated in Dallas, Texas. Since this event, there _____

many theories about what _____ on that fateful day.

According to the official U.S. government report, only one man

_____ the bullets that _____ President

Kennedy. However, even today many people _____ that

there _____ several assassins.

ACTIVITY 3

Fill in the blanks with the correct form of any appropriate verb.

Example Paragraph 10

A Routine Routine

I have one of the most boring daily routines of anyone I

_____ . Every morning, I _____ at 7:15.1

_____ a shower and _____ dressed.

After that, I _____ breakfast and _____

to the office. I _____ from 8:30 to 4:30. Then I

_____ home. This _____ five days a week

without fail. Just for once, I wish something different would happen!

Fill in the blanks with the correct form of the verbs in parentheses.

Example Paragraph 11

The Shortest Term in the White House

William Henry Harrison (be) _____ the ninth president of the United States. His presidency was extremely brief. In fact, Harrison (be) _____ president for only one month. He (take) _____ office on March 4,1841. Unfortunately he (catch) _____ a cold that (become) _____ pneumonia. On April 4, Harrison (die) _____ . He (become) _____ the first American president to die while in office. Before becoming president, Harrison (study) _____ to become a doctor and later (serve) _____ in the army.

ACTIVITY 5

Fill in the blanks with the correct form of the verbs in parentheses.

Example Paragraph 12

The History of Brownsville

Brownsville, Texas, is a city with an interesting history. Brownsville (be) _____ originally a fort during the Mexican-American War. During that war, American and Mexican soldiers (fight) _____ several battles in the area around the city. As a matter of fact, the city (get) _____ its name from Major Jacob Brown, an American soldier who was killed in a battle near the old fort. However, Brownsville's history (be) _____ not only connected to war. After the war, the city was best known for farming. The area's rich soil (help) _____ it become a thriving agriculture center. Over time, the agricultural industry (grow) _____ , and today Brownsville farmers (be) _____ well-known for growing cotton and citrus. In sum, both the Mexican-American War and farming have played important historical roles in making Brownsville such an interesting city.

Articles

Fill in the blanks with the correct article. If no article is required, write an X in the blank.

Example Paragraph 13

_____ Simple Math Problem

There is _____ interesting mathematics brainteaser that always amazes _____ people when they first hear it. First, pick _____ number from _____ 1 to _____ 9. Subtract _____ 5. (You may have a negative number.) Multiply this answer by _____ 3. Now square _____ number. Then add _____ digits of _____ number. For _____ example, if your number is 81, add 8 and 1 to get an answer of _____ 9. If _____ number is less than _____ 5, add _____ 5. If _____ number is not less than _____ 5, subtract _____ 4. Now multiply this number by _____ 2. Finally, subtract _____ 6. If you have followed _____ steps correctly, _____ your answer is _____ 4.

Fill in the blanks with the correct article. If no article is required, write an X in the blank.

Example Paragraph 14

_____ Geography Problems among _____ American Students

Are _____ American high school students _____ less educated in _____ geography than high school students in _____ other countries? According to _____ recent survey of _____ high school students all over _____ globe, _____ U.S. students do not know very much about _____ geography. For _____

example, _____ surprisingly large number did not know

_____ capital of _____ state in which

they live. Many could not find _____ Mexico on a map

even though Mexico is one of _____ two countries

that share _____ border with _____

United States. Some _____ educators blame this lack of

_____ geographical knowledge on the move away from

memorization of material that has taken _____ place

in _____ recent years in American schools. Regardless

of _____ cause, the unfortunate fact appears to be that

American _____ high school students are not learning

enough about this subject area.

Fill in the blanks with the correct article. If no article is required, write an X in the blank.

Example Paragraph 15

_____ Homeowners Saving _____ Money with a New Free Service

People who are concerned that their monthly electricity

bill is too high can now take _____ advantage of

_____ special free service offered by the local electricity

company. _____ company will do _____

home energy audit on any house to find out if _____

house is wasting _____ valuable energy. Homeowners

can call _____ power company to schedule _____

convenient time for _____ energy analyst to visit

their home. The audit takes only about _____ hour.

_____ analyst will inspect _____

home and identify potential energy-saving _____

improvements. For _____ example, he or she will

check _____ thermostat, the air-conditioning, and

_____ seals around doors and windows. The major

energy-use _____ problems will be identified, and

_____ analyst will recommend _____

ways to use _____ energy more efficiently.

Fill in the blanks with the correct article. If no article is required, write an X in the blank.

Example Paragraph 16

_____ Great Teacher

To this day, I am completely convinced that _____ main reason that I did so well in my French class in _____ high school was the incredible teacher that I had, _____ Mrs. Montluzin. I had not studied _____ foreign language before I started _____ Mrs. Montluzin's French class. _____ idea of being able to communicate in a foreign language, especially _____ French, intrigued me, but _____ idea also scared me. _____ French seemed so difficult at first. We had so much _____ vocabulary to memorize, and we had to do _____ exercises to improve our grammar. While it is true that there was _____ great deal of work to do, _____ Mrs. Montluzin always tried her best to make French class very interesting. She also gave us _____ suggestions for learning _____ French, and these helped me a lot. Since this French class, I have studied a few other languages, and my interest in _____ foreign languages today is due to _____ success I had in French class with _____ Mrs. Montluzin.

Fill in the blanks with the correct article. If no article is required, write an X in the blank.

Example Paragraph 17

_____ Surprising Statistics on _____ Higher Education in _____ United States

Although _____ United States is a leader in many areas, it is surprising that _____ number of Americans with _____ college degree is not as high as it is in some _____ other countries. Only about 22 percent of

_____ Americans have attended college for four or more

years. To _____ most people, this rather low ratio of one

in five is shocking. Slightly more than _____ 60 percent

of _____ Americans between _____

ages of 25 and 40 have taken some _____ college classes.

Though these numbers are far from what _____ many

people would expect in _____ United States, these

statistics are _____ huge improvement over figures

at _____ turn of _____ last century.

In _____ 1900, only about _____ 8

percent of all Americans even entered _____ college. At

_____ present time, there are about 21 million students

attending _____ college.

Editing for Errors

ACTIVITY 11

This paragraph contains eight errors. They are in word choice (one), article (one), modal* (one), verb tense (one), subject-verb agreement (three), and word order (one). Mark these errors and write the corrections above the errors.

Example Paragraph 18

A Dangerous Driving Problem

Imagine that you are driving your car home from mall or the library. You come to a bend in the road. You decide that you need to slow down a little, so you tap the brake pedal. Much to your surprise, the car does not begin to slow down. You push the brake pedal all the way down to the floor, but still anything happens. There are a few things you can do when your brakes does not work. One was to pump the brakes. If also this fails, you should to try the emergency brake. If this also fail, you should try to shift the car into a lower gear and rub the tires against the curb until the car come to a stop.

*Modals are *can, should, will, must, may,* and *might.* Modals appear before verbs. We do not use *to* between modals and verbs. (*Incorrect:* I should to go with him. *Correct:* I should go with him.) Modals do not have forms that take *-s, -ing,* or *-ed.*

This paragraph contains ten errors. They are in prepositions (three), word order (one), articles (two), and verb tense (four). Mark these errors and write the corrections above the errors.

Example Paragraph 19

The Start of My Love of Aquariums

My love of aquariums began a long time ago. Although I got my first fish when I am just seven years old, I can still remember the store, the fish, and salesclerk who waited on me that day. Because I made good grades on my report card, my uncle has rewarded me with a dollar. A few days later, I was finally able to go to the local dime store for spend my money. It was 1965, and dollar could buy a lot. I looked a lot of different things, but I finally chose to buy a fish. We had an old fishbowl at home, so it seems logical with me to get a fish. I must have spent 15 minutes pacing back and forth in front of all the aquariums before I finally choose my fish. It was a green swordtail, or rather, she was a green swordtail. A few weeks later, she gave birth to 20 or 30 baby swordtails. Years later, I can still remember the fish beautiful that got me so interested in aquariums.

This paragraph contains eight errors. They are in prepositions (one), articles (three), word forms (two), verb tense (one), and subject-verb agreement (one). Mark these errors and write the corrections above the errors.

Example Paragraph 20

An Effect of Cellphones on Drivers

Cellular phones, can be threat to safety. A recent study for Donald Redelmeier and Robert Tibshirani of the University of Toronto showed that cellular phones pose a risk to drivers. In fact, people who talk on the phone while driving are four time more likely to have an automobile accident than those who do not use the phone while drive. The Toronto researchers studied 699 drivers who had been in an automobile accident while they were using their cellular phones. The researchers concluded that the main reason for the accidents is not that people used one hand for the telephone and only one for driving. Rather, cause of the accidents was usually that the drivers became distracted, angry, or upset by the phone call. The drivers then lost concentration and was more prone to a car accident.

This paragraph contains seven errors. They are in verb tense (one), articles (two), word forms (three), and subject-verb agreement (one). Mark these errors and write the corrections.

Problems with American Coins

Many foreigners who come to the United States have very hard time getting used to America coins. The denominations of the coins are one, five, ten, 25, and 50 cents, and one dollar. However, people used only the first four regularly. The smallest coin in value is the penny, but it is not the smallest coin in size. The quarter is one-fourth the value of a dollar, but it is not one-fourth as big as a dollar. There is a dollar coin, but no one ever use it. In fact, perhaps the only place to find one is at a bank. All of the coins are silver-colored except for one, the penny. Finally, because value of each coin is not clearly written on the coin as it is in many country, foreigners often experience problems with monetarily transactions.

This paragraph contains seven errors. They are in word order (one), articles (two), preposition (one), subject-verb agreement (one), and verb tense (two). Mark these errors and write the corrections.

An Oasis of Silence

Life on this campus can be extremely hectic, so when I want the solitude, I go usually to the fourth floor of the library. The fourth floor has nothing but shelves and shelves of rare books and obscure periodicals. Because there are only a few small tables with some rather uncomfortable wooden chairs and no copy machines in this floor, few people are staying here very long. Students search for a book or periodical, found it, and then take it to a more sociable floor to photocopy the pages or simply browse through the articles. One of my best friends have told me that he does not like this floor that is so special to me. For him, it is a lonely place. For me, however, it is oasis of silence in a land of turmoil, a place where I can read, think, and write in peace.

Useful Vocabulary for Better Writing

These useful words and phrases can help you write better sentences and paragraphs. They can make your writing sound more academic, natural, and fluent.

Giving and Adding Examples

Words and Phrases	Examples
For example, S + V / *For instance,* S + V	Our reading teacher assigns a lot of homework. *For example*, last night we had to read ten pages and write an essay.
The first reason + VERB	The article we read in class gave three reasons that our planet is in trouble. *The first reason* is about the increasing population.

Concluding Sentences

Words and Phrases	Examples
In conclusion, S + V	*In conclusion,* I believe everyone should vote in every election.
By doing all of these things, S + V	*By doing all of these things,* we can improve education in our country.
Because of this, S + V	*Because of this,* many people will have better health care.
As a result, S + V	*As a result,* I chose to go to college in France instead of my country.
For these reasons, S + V	*For these reasons,* I prefer to eat at home instead of a restaurant.
In sum, S + V / *In summary,* S + V / *To summarize ,* S + V	*In sum,* World War II was a very complicated war with many countries fighting for very different reasons, but in many ways, it was a continuation of World War I.
In other words, S + V	*In other words,* the judge made an incorrect decision.
From the information given, we can conclude that S + V	*From the information given, we can conclude that* Mark Johnson is certainly the best soccer player in this decade.
It is clear that S + V	*It is clear that* exercising every day improved your health.

Comparing

Words and Phrases	Examples
NOUN *is* COMPARATIVE ADJECTIVE *than* NOUN	New York *is larger than* Rhode Island.
S + V + COMPARATIVE ADVERB *than* Y.	The cats ran *faster than* the dogs.
S + V. *In comparison,* S + V.	Canada has provinces. *In comparison,* Brazil has states.
Although NOUN *and* NOUN *are similar in* NOUN, S + V	*Although* France *and* Spain *are similar in* size, they are different in many ways.
NOUN *and* NOUN *are similar.*	Brazil *and* the United States *are* surprisingly *similar.*
NOUN *is the same*	Our house *is the same* size as your house.
…as ADJECTIVE *as…*	Our house is *as big as* your house.
Like NOUN, NOUN *also*	*Like* Brazil, Mexico *also* has states.
both NOUN *and* NOUN…	*In both* German *and* Japanese, the verb appears at the end of a sentence.

	The blooms on the red roses last longer than most other flowers. *Likewise*, the blooms for the pink rose are long-lasting.
Likewise, S + V / *Also*, S + V	
Similarly, S + V …/ *Similar to* NOUN	Economists believe India has a bright future. *Similarly*, Brazil's future is on a very positive track.

Contrasting

Words and Phrases	Examples
S + V. *In contrast*, S + V.	*Algeria* is a very large country. *In contrast*, the UAE is very small.
Contrasted with / *In contrast to* NOUN	*In contrast to* last year, our company has doubled its profits this year.
Although / *Even though* / *Though* S + V	*Although* Spain and France are similar in size, they are different in many other ways.
Unlike NOUN,	*Unlike* the pink roses, the red roses are very expensive.
However, S + V	Canada has provinces. *However*, Brazil has states.
On the one hand, S + V *On the other hand*, S + V	*On the one hand*, Maggie loved to travel. *On the other hand*, she hated to be away from her home.
The opposite S + V	Most of the small towns in my state are experiencing a boom in tourism. In my hometown, *the opposite* is true.
NOUN *and* NOUN *are different.*	My older brother *and* my younger brother *are very different*.

Telling a Story / Narrating

Words and Phrases	Examples
When I was X, I would VERB	*When I was* a child, *I would* go fishing every weekend.
I have never felt so ADJ *in my life.*	*I have never felt so* anxious *in my life*.
I will never forget NOUN	*I will never forget* the day I took my first international flight.
I can still remember NOUN / *I will always remember* NOUN	*I can still remember* the day I started my first job.
NOUN *was the best / worst day of my life.*	My wedding was *the best day of my life*.
Every time X happened, Y happened.	*Every time* I used that computer, I had a problem.
This was my first …	*This was my first* job after graduating from college.

Describing a Process

Words and Phrases	Examples
First (Second, Third, etc.), … *Next*, … *After that*, …*Then*, … *Finally*, …	*First*, I cut the apples into small pieces. *Next*, I added some mayonnaise. *After that*, I added some salt. *Finally*, I mixed everything together well.
The first thing you should do is VERB	*The first thing you should do is* turn on the computer.
VERB+*-ing requires you to follow (number) of steps.*	*Saving* a file on a computer *requires you to follow several simple steps*.
Before you VERB, *you should* VERB.	*Before you* write a paragraph, *you should* brainstorm for ideas.
After (When)…	*After* you brainstorm your ideas, you can select the best ones to write about in your essay.

After that, …	After that, you can select the best ones to write about in your essay.
The last step is… / Finally, …	Finally, you should cook all of the ingredients for an hour.
If you follow these important steps in VERB + -ing,…	If you follow these important steps in applying for a passport, you will have your new document in a very short time.

Defining

Words and Phrases	Examples
The NOUN, which is a/an NOUN + ADJECTIVE CLAUSE, MAIN VERB	An owl, which is a bird that has huge round eyes, is awake most of the night.
According to the dictionary…	According to The Collins Cobuild Dictionary of American English, gossip is "an informal conversation, often about people's private affairs."
The dictionary definition of NOUN	The dictionary definition of gumbo is not very good.
X released a report stating that S + V	The president's office released a report stating that the new law will require all adults between the ages of 18 and 30 to serve at least one year of active military duty.
In other words, S + V	In other words, we have to redo everything we have done so far.
,…which means…	The paper is due tomorrow, which means if you want to get a good grade, you need to finish it today.
NOUN means…	Gossip means talking or writing about other people's private affairs.

Showing Cause and Effect

Words and Phrases	Examples
Because of NOUN, S + V. Because S + V, S + V.	Because of the traffic problems, it is easy to see why the city is building a new tunnel.
NOUN can trigger NOUN. NOUN can cause NOUN.	An earthquake can trigger tidal waves and can cause massive destruction.
Due to NOUN, …	Due to the snowstorm, all schools will be closed tomorrow.
As a result of NOUN…	As a result of his efforts, he got a better job.
Therefore,…/ As a result,…/ For this reason,…/ Consequently,…	It suddenly began to rain. Therefore, we all got wet.
NOUN will bring about …	The use of the Internet will bring about a change in education.
NOUN has had a good / bad effect on…	Computer technology has had both positive and negative effects on society.
The correlation is clear / evident.	The correlation between junk food and obesity is clear.

Describing

Words and Phrases	Examples
Prepositions of location: *above, across, around, in the dark, near, under…*	The children raced their bikes *around* the school.
Descriptive adjectives: *wonderful, delightful, dangerous, informative, rusty…*	The *bent, rusty* bike squeaked when I rode it.
SUBJECT *is* ADJECTIVE.	This dictionary *is informative*.
X is the most ADJECTIVE + NOUN.	To me, Germany *is the most interesting* country in Europe.
X tastes / looks / smells / feels like NOUN.	My ID card *looks like* a credit card.
X is known / famous for its NOUN.	France *is known for* its cheese.

Stating an Opinion

Words and Phrases	Examples
Without a doubt, VERB *is* ADJECTIVE *idea / method / decision / way.*	*Without a doubt,* walking to work each day *is* an excellent *way* to lose weight.
Personally, I believe/think/feel/agree/ disagree/ suppose S + V.	*Personally, I believe that* smoking on a bus should not be allowed.
VERB+*-ing should not be allowed.*	Smoking in public *should not be allowed.*
In my opinion/ view/ experience, NOUN	*In my opinion,* smoking is rude.
For this reason, S + V. / *That is why I think…*	I do not have a car. *For this reason,* I do not care about rising gasoline prices.
There are many benefits / advantages to NOUN.	*There are many benefits to* swimming every day.
There are many drawbacks / disadvantages to NOUN.	*There are many drawbacks to* eating your meals at a restaurant.
I am convinced that S + V	*I am convinced that* education at a university should be free to all citizens.
NOUN *should be required / mandatory.*	College *should be required.*
I prefer NOUN *to* NOUN.	*I prefer* soccer to football.
To me, banning / prohibiting NOUN *makes (perfect) sense.*	*To me, banning* cell phones while driving *makes perfect sense.*
For all of these important reasons, I think / believe / feel (that) S + V	*For all of these important reasons, I think* smoking *should be* banned in public.
Based on X, I have come to the conclusion that S + V	*Based on* two books that I read recently, *I have come to the conclusion that* global warming is the most serious problem that my generation faces.

Arguing and Persuading

Words and Phrases	Examples
It is important to remember that S + V	*It is important to remember* that school uniforms would only be worn during school hours.
According to a recent survey, S + V	*According to a recent survey,* 85 percent of high school students felt they had too much homework.
Even more important, S + V	*Even more important,* statistics show the positive effects that school uniforms have on behavior.
Despite this, S + V	The report says this particular kind of airplane is dangerous. *Despite this,* the government has not banned this airplane.
SUBJECT *must / should / ought to* VERB	Researchers *must* stop unethical animal testing.
The reason for S + V	*The reason for* people's support of this plan is that it provides equal treatment for all citizens.
To emphasize, S + V	*To emphasize,* I support a lower age for voting but only for those who already have a high school diploma.
For these reasons, S + V	*For these reasons,* public schools should require uniforms.
Obviously, S + V	*Obviously,* there are many people who would disagree with what I have just said.
Without a doubt, S + V	*Without a doubt,* students ought to learn a foreign language.
I agree that S + V. *However* S + V	*I agree that* a college degree is important. *However,* getting a practical technical license can also be very useful.

Reacting/Responding

Words and Phrases	Examples
TITLE *by* AUTHOR *is a / an…*	*Harry Potter and the Goblet of Fire by* J.K. Rowling *is an* entertaining book to read.
My first reaction to the prompt / news / article was / is NOUN.	*My first reaction to the article was* fear.
When I read / look at / think about NOUN, I was amazed / shocked / surprised …	*When I read* the article, *I was surprised* to learn of his athletic ability.